P9-CAR-413

PRACTICALLY USELESS INFORMATION™
FOOD & DRINK

Also in the
PRACTICALLY USELESS INFORMATION™
Series:

♥

Weddings

PRACTICALLY USELESS INFORMATION™

FOOD & DRINK

A Kolpas Compendium™

Norman Kolpas

RUTLEDGE HILL PRESS
Nashville, Tennessee
A Division of Thomas Nelson Publishers
Since 1798

www.thomasnelson.com

Copyright © 2005 by Kolpas Media Inc.

"Practically Useless Information" and "Kolpas Compendium" are registered trademarks of Kolpas Media Inc.

All rights reserved. No portion of this book may be reproduced, stored in a retrieval system, or transmitted in any form or by any means—electronic, mechanical, photocopy, recording, or any other—except for brief quotations in printed reviews, without prior permission of the publisher.

Published by Rutledge Hill Press, a Division of Thomas Nelson, Publishers, P.O. Box 141000, Nashville, Tennessee 37214.

Rutledge Hill Press books may be purchased in bulk for educational, business, fundraising, or sales promotional use. For information, please e-mail SpecialMarkets@ThomasNelson.com.

Design by Gore Studio Inc.

Library of Congress Cataloging-in-Publication Data

Kolpas, Norman.
    Practically useless information. Food & drink / Norman Kolpas.
       p. cm.—(Practically useless information)
    Includes bibliographical references and index.
    ISBN 1-4016-0205-3 (hardcover)
      1. Food—Miscellanea. 2. Beverages—Miscellanea. I. Title: Food & drink. II Title. III. Series.

TX355.K66 2005
641—dc22

                            2004024326

Printed in the United States of America

05 06 07 08 09—5 4 3 2 1

FOR KATIE & JAKE

We should look for someone to eat and drink with
before looking for something to eat and drink, for dining
alone is leading the life of a lion or wolf.
—*Aphorisms* (ca. 300 BC), Epicurus

Some Acknowledgments

The creation of any book is like a dinner party: Most of the time, one person does the cooking. But the event only becomes a true success through the enthusiastic participation of the other people seated around the table, not to mention those who pitch in afterwards to help clean up!

With that in mind, so many people have helped to make this book a memorable experience. First, thanks go to everyone at Rutledge Hill Press and Thomas Nelson for being such delightful participants. Larry Stone and Bryan Curtis saw merit in the idea from the start; so, too, did David Dunham, who so graciously introduced me to his colleagues at Thomas Nelson including Pamela Clements, Rutledge Hill's new associate publisher. Jennifer Greenstein kept things flowing calmly and smoothly as editor, and Geoff Stone, Tracey Menges, Tina Goodrow, and Halley Davis provided steady help along the way. Thanks also to copy editor Sara Henry for fine-tuning the text, to designer Bruce Gore for making it look terrrific, to typesetter Lindsay Carreker for her detailed care, and to proofreaders Norma Bates and Denver Sherry for their keen eyes.

My wife, Katie, and our son, Jake, deserve the greatest thanks of all. Their enthusiasm for sharing the pleasures of the table gives me wonderful support, and has contributed immeasurably to this book.

Introduction

Whenever I pick up a cooking or wine magazine or a newspaper food section, I don't read the articles first. I realize that's a serious admission to make from someone who writes feature articles, but there it is.

What draws me first aren't lengthy stories, or even the beautiful pictures of prepared meals or of fine wines shimmering in delicate crystal. Rather, I go straight to the sidebars, those tinted boxes that feature definitions of terms, interesting statistics, oddball facts, or lists suggesting what you, the reader, should order when perusing a particular menu.

And I know I'm not the only one who reads the sidebars first. Not by a long shot.

Back in the mid-1970s, I was working in London for a big international publishing company that produced series of beautifully illustrated nonfiction books. After completing my assignments on a nature series, for which I wrote and edited essays—about such topics as the birds of paradise that lived in New Guinea's rainforests, nature preserves in Poland, and the wildflowers that bloomed from the desert sands once every seven years when rain finally fell in the Australian Outback—I was assigned, junior staffer that I was, to work on the preliminary development for what became a 30-plus-volume how-to cooking series. Once it got the go-ahead, I stayed on the series for four and a half years and thus I acquired an extensive education in food and wine.

During my time with this company, I recall seeing a survey of reading habits our parent corporation conducted of its customers—not just the buyers of the cooking series, but also those who bought books from them on nature, travel, art, history, and other topics meant to build home libraries. With so many years gone by now, I don't remember the precise figures, but they were something like this: Only 5 percent of the buyers actually read the text that made up about half of each book; another 20 percent read the short-article-length texts of the photo essays that punctuated each chapter; and a good 75 percent only looked at the pictures or charts and read the detailed captions that went with them.

In short, most people go for the sidebars first.

So, I thought, why not create a book for food and drink enthusiasts composed exclusively of sidebar material, doing away with all that pesky text you normally try and fail to read, continuously and in order, from front cover to last?

That's the genesis for the volume you now hold in your hands. I've devised it with one simple goal in mind: to be a book on food and drink that you don't really need, but one you'll find virtually impossible to put down.

The contents are entirely arbitrary, dictated solely by the kind of oddball stuff that fascinates me and is likely to draw my attention. Flip through these pages and you'll find what I hope you'll think of as a delightful hodgepodge assortment of culinary and potable information:

❧ Lists of unusual frozen dessert flavors for sale in Japan (page 123) and others developed in the United States for special offers on April Fool's Day (page 116)

❧ Detailed instructions on how to slice a banana without removing or cutting its peel (page 48)

❧ Glossaries of classic American diner slang (pages 92–94) and food terms from Britain's Cockney rhyming slang (pages 42–45)

❧ A guide to some well-known dishes named after famous people (page 130–131).

You get the idea: It's the sort of useless information that so many people really can't live without.

Of course, if you actually can't live without something, it must have some practical value to you as well; hence, this book's label, "*Practically Useless Information.*" I can imagine instances where it might be of some use to you to know about squid ice cream, or what a waitress means when she tells the short-order cook to "wreck 'em," or why you might want to play a prank on someone by placing a trick banana in a bowlful of whole fruit.

I've even included, scattered throughout these pages, information to which the word "practical" might even more readily apply:

❧ Conversion tables for imperial and metric cooking measurements (pages 48–49, 84, and 118)

❧ Doneness temperatures for meats and poultry (page 79)

❧ A chart of suggested refrigerator and freezer storage times for various kinds of foods (pages 150–153).

And, because I'm a passionately devoted reader who is still trying to draw practical value from a bachelor's degree in English literature, you'll also find a generous scattering of literary excerpts and quotes from sources as varied as the Bible, Charles Dickens, Henry David Thoreau, William Shakespeare, Beatrix Potter, Edgar Allan Poe, Honoré de Balzac, Mark Twain, and Alice B. Toklas. You might be amazed, and will likely be delighted, by how much creative attention great writers have paid to the topics of food and drink.

Not that I have included anything in this book just because I consider it practical. Rather, I just find such information interesting, and all the more so when it is juxtaposed with the food-and-drink-related dying words of famous people, or competitive eating records, or lists of place names you're more likely to find in your shopping cart than on the map.

So think of this book much as you would a buffet or an open bar: an opportunity to graze, sampling lots of different foods and drinks that you might fancy. The goal is, first, to amuse and tantalize you,then, perhaps, even to satisfy you and maybe even intoxicate you.

The offerings are vast and varied. Please dig in and enjoy yourself.

JOHN HEYWOOD'S FOOD AND DRINK PROVERBS

Selections from the *Proverbs* compiled and published around 1546 by the English playwright, poet, and epigrammatist:

A man may well bring a horse to water,
but he cannot make him drink.

◆

Butter would not melt in her mouth.

◆

Drink away sorrow.

◆

God never sendeth mouth but he sendeth meat.

◆

Half a loaf is better than none.

◆

Out of the frying pan into the fire.

◆

She is neither fish, nor flesh, nor good red herring.

◆

The fat is in the fire.

◆

The moon is made of green cheese.

◆

Would ye both eat your cake and have your cake?

A FINE ENGLISH PICNIC BASKET INDEED

"What's inside it?" asked the Mole, wriggling with curiosity.

"There's cold chicken inside it," replied the Rat briefly; "coldtonguecoldhamcoldbeefpickledgherkinssaladfrenchrollscressandwidgespottedmeatgingerbeerlemonadesodawater–"

"Oh stop, stop," cried the Mole in ecstasies: "This is too much!"

"Do you really think so?" inquired the Rat seriously. "It's only what I always take on these little excursions; and the other animals are always telling me that I'm a mean beast and cut it *very* fine!"

—*The Wind in the Willows* (1908), Kenneth Grahame

THE POETRY OF FRUIT CULTIVARS

An arbitrary selection of evocative names for common fruits' cultivars (specific varieties established and maintained through cultivation):

Apple: Empire, Gala, Golden Delicious, Fireside, Honeycrisp, Honeygold, Jonalicious, Liberty, Red Delicious, Redfree, Spartan, Suncrisp, Wealthy.

Apricot: Cluthearly, Goldcot, Goldrich, Goldstrike, Haroblush, Harogem, Rival, Velvaglo, Vivagold.

Banana: Giant Governor, Praying Hands, Thousand Fingers.

Blackberry: Apache, Arapaho, Black Satin, Cherokee, Illinois Hardy, Kiowa, Loganberry, Navaho, Shawnee, Smoothstem, Tayberry, Triple Crown.

Black Currant: August Reward, Beauty of Altay, Coronation, Crusader, Goliath, Mopsy, Onyx, Rain-in-the-Face, Raven, Tinker, Topsy, White Eagle.

Blueberry: Aurora, Berkeley, Bluecrop, Blueray, Bluetta, Bluejay, Chippewa, Darrow, Duke, Earlblue, Elliott, Liberty, Patriot, Spartan.

Cherry: Bing, Cashmere, Cavalier, Cristalina, Galaxy, Glacier, Index, Meteor, Northstar, Olympus, Rainier, Sonata, Sweetheart, Venus, Viscount.

Gooseberry: Abundance, Achilles, Captivator, Careless, Gem, Jubilee Careless, Pixwell, Poorman, Speedwell, Surprise, Telegraph, White Lion.

Kiwifruit: Ananasnaja, Blake, Dumbarton Oaks, Hayward, Issai, Matua, Red Princess, Saanichton 12, Tomuri.

Mango: Banana, Bullock's Heart, Parrot Mango, Sensation.

Papaya: Baixinho, Higgins, Honey Gold, Solo, Sunrise Solo, Wilder.

Peach: Allstar, Blazingstar, Coralstar, Earliglo, Flamin Fury, Garnet Beauty, Golden Monarch, Jerseyglo, Redhaven, Redkist, Sunhaven, Vanity, Vivid.

Pear: Anjou, Bartlett, Comice, Duchess, Flemish Beauty, Moon Glow.

Pineapple: Bull Head, Charlotte Rothschild, Congo Red, Egyptian Queen, Hilo, Pearl, Queen, Red Spanish, Smooth Cayenne, Sugarloaf.

Plum: Blue Imperial, Blueball, Climax, Compass, Crescent, Grand Duke, Monarch, Pride, Redglow, Silver Prune, White Egg, Yellow Egg.

Raspberry: Autumn Bliss, Brandywine, Centennial, Chilliwack, Emily, Encore, Fall Gold, Heritage, Jewel, Killarney, Meeker, Prelude, Royalty, Summit, Titan.

Red currant: Cherry, Earliest of Fourlands, Perfection, Red Lake, Redstart, White Imperial, Wilder.

Strawberry: Allstar, Avalon, Earlyglow, Evangeline, Everest, Honeoye, Jewel, L'Amour, Ovation, Sable, Sapphire, Seascape, Serenity, Tribute, Tristar.

TEN CLASSIC DIM SUM VARIETIES

Go to a Chinese restaurant specializing in dim sum, the morning or lunchtime tea snacks whose name translates roughly as "delight the heart," and you'll encounter a possibly bewildering array of steamed, baked, fried, or boiled treats. Fortunately, diners are encouraged to point and ask. This glossary of a few classics, however, will get you started and provide a satisfying first foray.

Bao: Fluffy steamed or baked dumpling, usually filled with *cha siu.*

Cha siu: Barbecued pork, used either as a filling for *bao* or *cheung fun*, or served on its own on a platter, sliced into bite-sized pieces.

Cheung fun: Sheets of translucent rice noodle, rolled up around a filling of shrimp, pork, or beef and then steamed.

Daan tat: Tartlets of flaky pastry encasing a rich, sweet egg custard filling.

Har kow: Plump, crescent-shaped steamed dumplings with a translucent wheat noodle wrapper enclosing a filling of shrimp and bamboo shoots.

Hua juan: Scallion "flower" rolls made by spreading a sheet of yeast-leavened dough with chopped scallions and sesame oil, rolling it up like a jellyroll, cutting it into slices, and steaming them.

Jiao zi: Steamed meatballs of beef or pork, often seasoned with ginger.

Nor mi gai: Plump bundles of sticky rice mixed with pork, sausage, chicken, shrimp, and mushrooms, steamed inside a lotus-leaf that perfumes the rice.

Siu mai: Steamed dumplings shaped like miniature teacups that usually contain a filling of minced pork and seasonings.

Wor tee: Also commonly called by their English name "potstickers," crescent-shaped wheat-noodle dumplings with a ground pork, chicken, or vegetable filling, cooked by a combination of pan-frying and steaming.

FROM THE RUBÁIYÁT

A Book of Verses underneath the Bough,
A Jug of Wine, a Loaf of Bread—and Thou
Beside me singing in the Wilderness—
Oh, Wilderness were Paradise enow!
    —Omar Khayyam (11th century AD),
translated by Edward FitzGerald (5th edition, 1879)

SOME NATIONAL FOOD OBSERVANCES: JANUARY

Usually by congressional or presidential declaration, a variety of foods and drinks have been honored with their own days of celebration. Here are the first month's honorees (more to follow throughout the book).

Entire month:
National Candy Month
National Hot Tea Month
National Oatmeal Month
National Soup Month
National Wheat Bread Month

1st: National Bloody Mary Day
2nd: National Cream Puff Day
3rd: National Chocolate-Covered Cherry Day
4th: National Spaghetti Day
5th: National Bean Day
National Whipped Cream Day
6th: National Shortbread Day
7th: National Tempura Day
8th: National English Toffee Day
9th: National Apricot Day
10th: National Bittersweet Chocolate Day
11th: National Milk Day
12th: National Marzipan Day
14th: National Hot Pastrami Sandwich Day
15th: National Strawberry Ice Cream Day
16th: National Fig Newton Day
17th: National Hot Buttered Rum Day
19th: National Popcorn Day
20th: National Buttercrunch Day
22nd: National Blonde Brownie Day
23rd: National Rhubarb Pie Day
24th: National Peanut Butter Day
26th: National Peanut Brittle Day
27th: National Chocolate Cake Day
28th: National Blueberry Pancake Day
29th: National Corn Chip Day
30th: National Croissant Day
31st: National Brandy Alexander Day

SIXTEENTH CENTURY TABLE MANNERS FOR CHILDREN

Excerpted from *De Civilitate Morum Puerilium* (*On Civility in Children*), published in 1530, by Dutch philosopher Desiderius Erasmus:

On Coming to Table:
Come to the table clean and in a merry mood.

◆

On Pausing Before Eating:
Some people immediately descend on the dishes the moment they have been set down. Wolves do that.

◆

On Banquet Settings:
At banquets, two people share each soup bowl and use squares of bread (trenchers) to serve as plates.

◆

On Letting Others Go First:
Be careful not to be the first to put your hands in the dish.

◆

On Avoiding Greediness:
What you cannot hold in your hands you must put on your plate.

◆

On Resting Your Hands:
Do not rest your hands on your trencher.

◆

On Drinking:
Do not drink more than two or three times during the meal (mostly wine diluted with water or thin beer), and wipe your lips with a napkin after each sip, especially if a common drinking-cup is used.

◆

On Food You Cannot Swallow:
Turn around discreetly and throw it somewhere.

◆

On Bones:
Do not put chewed bones back on plates.
Instead, throw them on the floor for the dog.

◆

On Licking Your Fingers:
It is impolite to lick greasy fingers or to wipe them on your coat. Better
to use the tablecloth or the serviette.

◆

On Burping:
Retain the wind by compressing the belly.

◆

On Sitting Still and Avoiding False Impressions:
Do not move back and forth on your chair. Doing so gives the impres-
sion of constantly breaking, or trying to break, wind.

◆

On Spitting:
Turn away lest your saliva fall on someone. If anything purulent
falls on the ground, tread upon it, lest it nauseate someone.

◆

On Sharing Your Handkerchief:
Do not offer your handkerchief to anyone unless
it has been freshly washed.

◆

On Losing Your Food:
Do not be afraid of vomiting if you must; it is not vomiting
but holding the vomit in your throat that is foul.

SOME MILESTONES IN FOOD AND DRINK HISTORY:
13TH TO 1ST CENTURIES BC

1275 BC: Led by Moses, Jews wandering in the Sinai survive on "manna,"
most likely a form of fungus or a sap exuded by tamarisk trees.

621 BC: Deuteronomy sets forth dietary restrictions for Jews (see pages
26–27).

350 BC: In Greece, Archestratus records recipes for steak and fish, among
others, in his poetic parody *Hydapathea (The Life of Luxury)*.

301 BC: The Greek philosopher Epicurus promotes the pleasures of food
and drink.

170 BC: The profession of baker originates in Rome.

110 BC: Near the future site of Naples, Romans first cultivate oyster beds.

69 BC: Cherries first arrive in Rome from the vicinity of the Black Sea.

48 BC: Back from campaigns in France and Britain, Julius Caesar brings
pork sausage-making to Rome.

JAPANESE BRAND-NAME INGENUITY

Actual Japanese packaged food and drink brands:

Air in Chocolate: Chocolate-coated bonbons with fluffy fruit centers.

Angel Relief: Chocolate-coated biscuits let you "listen to the Angel's whisper."

Baked Chunk: Biscuits studded with whole cashew nuts.

Beer Choco: Beer-flavored chocolate, "the confectionery of the bitter taste."

BlackBlack: Chewing gum with "Hi-technical excellent taste and flavor."

Blendy: Bottled coffee.

Boss: Canned coffee drinks in flavors including "On Business," "Fine Roast," "Café au Lait," and "Intermission."

Crack Up: Soft tropical fruit-flavored candy.

Creap: Powdered coffee creamer.

Crunky: Crunchy chocolate bar.

Cubyrop: Fruit-flavored hard candies.

Deep Sea Water: From the Murato Deep Sea, "shielded from the sunlight and atmospheric air"; "Gentle to your system, it keeps you in good health."

Eat me! Strawberry-coconut pudding cups.

Ethnican Chips: Barbecue-flavored potato chips.

Eye Power: Sugarless blueberry candy.

Fireman: Chewing gum with a "burning orange" flavor.

Football Salami: Beef jerky shaped like a football.

Gettin' Cool: Fruit-flavored sodas.

Hacker: Mint and grapefruit candy.

Hello Panda: "Tasty biscuits with creamy chocolate filling."

Let's Quiq: Fast-cooking rice mixes.

Meltyblend: White-chocolate candy.

Pocari Sweat: Energy drink.

Qoo!: Orange juice drink.

Slash: "White mint" chewing gum that promises to "shock your mouth."

Slow Life Stew: Stew sauce mixes.

Super Brain Panic: A "blue cola" chewing gum.

Vermont Curry: New England–style curry "with a touch of apple and honey."

Vessel in the Fog: Foamy chocolate candy bar.

Watering KissMint: Chewing gum.

Wow: Cola brand bills itself as, "Not gorgeous, not snobbish, not expensive."

RAVISHED BY MELONS

What aroma do I sense in this room?
What amber and musk sweet perfume
Enters my brain to delight
And my heart to excite?
Oh! Good God! I fall into an ecstatic haze:
Would viewing beautiful flowers in this vase
On top of this buffet
Produce in me an effect so intense?
Has someone burned sweet incense?

*   *   *

No, I do not think it can be any of those
Things that you to me propose.
What is it then? It is something I have seen
In this basket overflowing with green:
It is a melon on which nature, like a glove,
Has engraved its surface with a thousand jottings of love
As a clear sign for everyone to eat
This soft and amiable treat.

*   *   *

Not the dear apricot of which I dream,
Nor the strawberry lavished with cream,
Nor the manna from heaven sent,
Nor honey pure as testament,
Nor the sacred pear of Tours,
Nor the sweet green fig's allure,
Nor the plum juicy and divine,
Nor the Muscat grape on the vine,
Are more to me than bitterness and mud
When this ravishing melon courses through my blood.

*   *   *

Oh living source of light, creator of all that is right,
Who sees and embraces all, on my knees to you I fall
In humble gratitude
For the gift of this heavenly food.

—"Le Melon" (ca. 1580), Marc Antoine de Saint-Amant

EATING AND DRINKING ACROSS THE MAP
PART I: PRODUCE DEPARTMENT

Let your eye wander over an atlas when you're hungry or thirsty, and you might be amazed by the place names that emerge.

Apple, Ohio (also Oklahoma)
Apple River, Nova Scotia, Canada
Apple Tree Creek, Queensland,
  Australia
Apple Tree Flat, New South
  Wales, Australia
Banana, Queensland, Australia
Banana Creek, Florida
Banana Hill, Mississippi
Cantaloupe, Indiana
Celeryville, Ohio
Chard, England
Cherry, Arizona (also Illinois,
  Minnesota, North Carolina,
  Tennessee, and West Virginia)
Cherry Gardens, South Australia
Cherry Gully, Queensland,
  Australia
Cherry Orchard, England
Cherry Tree, England
Cherry Tree Hill, New South
  Wales, Australia
Cherryville, South Australia
Coconut, Florida
Garlic Creek, Texas
Garlic Island, Michigan
Garlic Mountain, Michigan
Grape, Arkansas (also California
  and Michigan)
Lemon, Kentucky (also Missis-
  sippi, Ohio, and Pennsylvania)
Lettuce Branch, North Carolina

Lettuce Creek, Florida
Lettuce Lake, California
  (also Florida)
Lime, Alabama (also Colorado
  and Oregon)
Mango, Florida
Melon, Texas
Mushroom Corner, Washington
Mushroom Farms, Pennsylvania
Nectarine, Pennsylvania
Okra, Tennessee
Onion Creek, Texas
  (also Washington)
Onion Lake, Saskatchewan,
  Canada
Onion Spring, Texas
Oniontown, New York (also
  Pennsylvania)
Orange, California
  (also Connecticut, Florida,
  Massachusetts, New Hampshire,
  New Jersey, Ohio, Pennsylvania,
  Texas, Virginia, and New South
  Wales, Australia)
Papaya Hammock, Florida
Peach, North Carolina
  (also Tennessee)
Pear Tree, England
Pearblossom, California
Pearland, Texas
Plum, Kentucky
  (also Pennsylvania and Texas)

Potato Island, New Jersey
Potato Mound, Indiana
Potato Patch, Arizona
(also New Mexico)
Pumpkin Bend, Alabama
Pumpkin Center, California (also
Alabama, Arizona, Florida,
North Carolina, and Oklahoma)
Rhubarb Pond, New Hampshire
Squash Hollow Brook, Connecticut
Squash Lake, Minnesota (also
Wisconsin)

Squash Pond, New York
Tangerine, Florida
Tomato, Arkansas
Watermelon Bay, Louisiana
Watermelon Branch, North Car-
olina (also Texas and South Car-
olina)
Watermelon Creek, Alabama
(also Georgia, New York,
Oregon, and South Carolina)

SYMBOLS IN HUMAN HISTORY

Food and drink have such intense emotional significance that they are often linked with events that have nothing to do with nutrition. The perpetrators of the Boston Tea Party were angry not over tea but over taxation; the breadline and apple-sellers of the Great Depression became symbols of what was wrong with the economy. Guests at a dinner party usually leave a little food on the plate to let their hosts know they have been fed to repletion. A child who misbehaves is sent to bed without dinner, while obedience is rewarded with candy or ice cream. The simple fact of sitting down to eat together may convey important statements about a society. The civil-rights movement in the southern United States during the 1950s began as a dispute about the right of blacks not simply to eat at lunch counters but to sit down there with whites; blacks insisted on that right because in North American society people sit down to eat only as equals.

—*Consuming Passions: The Anthropology of Eating* (1980),
Peter Farb and George Armelagos

RANDOM STATS, PART I: BOTTLED WATER

8: Number of eight-ounce daily servings of water recommended for a healthy adult.
4.6: Daily servings of water the average American adult drinks.
1 in 10: American adults who report drinking no water daily.

A DICKENS OF A PUDDING

No novelist captured the very heart of English life, certainly in the Victorian period and perhaps at any time, better than Charles Dickens (1812–1870)—and not least in his scenes centering on food and drink. This fact may be seen particularly well through the attention he pays to the Great British culinary concept of the pudding: a boiled savory or sweet dish enjoyed by working class and gentry alike.

Nicholas Nickleby (1838–1839)
'Why, then I'll tell you what,' rejoined the landlord. 'There's a gentleman in the parlour that's ordered a hot beef-steak pudding and potatoes, at nine. There's more of it than he can manage, and I have very little doubt that if I ask leave, you can sup with him. I'll do that, in a minute.'

A Christmas Carol (1843)
But now, the plates being changed by Miss Belinda, Mrs Cratchit left the room alone—too nervous to bear witnesses—to take the pudding up and bring it in.

Suppose it should not be done enough? Suppose it should break in turning out? Suppose somebody should have got over the wall of the back–yard, and stolen it, while they were merry with the goose—a supposition at which the two young Cratchits became livid. All sorts of horrors were supposed.

Hallo! A great deal of steam. The pudding was out of the copper. A smell like a washing-day! That was the cloth. A smell like an eating-house and a pastrycook's next door to each other, with a laundress's next door to that! That was the pudding. In half a minute Mrs Cratchit entered—flushed, but smiling proudly—with the pudding, like a speckled cannon-ball, so hard and firm, blazing in half of half-a-quartern of ignited brandy, and bedight with Christmas holly stuck into the top.

Oh, a wonderful pudding. Bob Cratchit said, and calmly too, that he regarded it as the greatest success achieved by Mrs Cratchit since their marriage. Mrs. Cratchit said that now the weight was off her mind, she would confess she had had her doubts about the quantity of flour. Everybody had something to say about it, but nobody said or thought it was at all a small pudding for a large family. It would have been flat heresy to do so. Any Cratchit would have blushed to hint at such a thing.

David Copperfield (1849–1850)

He brought me a pudding, and having set it before me, seemed to ruminate, and to become absent in his mind for some moments.

'How's the pie?' he said, rousing himself.

'It's a pudding,' I made answer.

'Pudding!' he exclaimed. 'Why, bless me, so it is! What!' looking at it nearer. 'You don't mean to say it's a batter-pudding!'

'Yes, it is indeed.'

'Why, a batter-pudding,' he said, taking up a table-spoon, 'is my favourite pudding! Ain't that lucky? Come on, little 'un, and let's see who'll get most.'

The waiter certainly got most. He entreated me more than once to come in and win, but what with his table-spoon to my tea-spoon, his dispatch to my dispatch, and his appetite to my appetite, I was left far behind at the first mouthful, and had no chance with him. I never saw anyone enjoy a pudding so much, I think; and he laughed, when it was all gone, as if his enjoyment of it lasted still.

"The Schoolboy's Story" (1853)

When they didn't give him boiled mutton, they gave him rice pudding, pretending it was a treat. And saved the butcher.

Great Expectations (1860–1861)

It was Christmas Eve, and I had to stir the pudding for next day, with a copper-stick, from seven to eight by the Dutch clock.

"Doctor Marigold" (1865)

I am a neat hand at cookery, and I'll tell you what I knocked up for my Christmas-eve dinner in the Library Cart. I knocked up a beefsteak-pudding for one, with two kidneys, a dozen oysters, and a couple of mushrooms thrown in. It's a pudding to put a man in good humour with everything, except the two bottom buttons of his waistcoat.

The Mystery of Edwin Drood (1869–1870)

Firstly, the Philanthropists were in very bad training: much too fleshy, and presenting, both in face and figure, a superabundance of what is known to Pugilistic Experts as Suet Pudding.

ADVENTURES IN ICE CREAM, PART I: AN ACADEMIC APPROACH

Established in 1917, the Dairy Store at the University of Nebraska's Lincoln campus gives aspiring student ice cream artisans the opportunity to learn how to make the best possible scoopable product and to develop innovative flavors. From the 200-plus flavors developed down through the years, some of the more out-of-the-ordinary creations could make those of the big-time multiple-flavor chains seem tame. (And that doesn't even begin to mention the outstanding student-made cheeses.)

* Amaretto Raspberry
* Anniversary Apple Cinnamon Pecan Pie
* Apple Strudel
* Bananas Foster
* Bavarian Mint
* Candy Corn
* Cantaloupe
* Chocolaty S'Mores
* Coffee Chocolate Chunk
* Cotton Candy
* 4-H Clover Mint (mint with chocolate)
* Jolly Rancher
* Karmel Kashew
* Lemon Custard
* Mango
* Margarita Sherbet
* Strawberry-Rhubarb
* Peanut Butter Chocolate Chip Chocolate
* Pumpkin Pie

FUN WITH FOOD & DRINK, PART I: HOW TO MAKE PEPPER DEFY GRAVITY

Static electricity makes simple ground pepper fly upward.

1. **Assemble your materials.** You will need finely ground black pepper, a plastic picnic-style spoon, a clean dry plate, and a piece of wool cloth. Spread some pepper on the plate.
2. **Rub the spoon.** For several seconds, vigorously rub the back of the spoon's bowl on the piece of wool. This will build a negative electrical charge on the spoon's surface.
3. **Hold the spoon over the pepper.** Immediately position the bottom of the spoon's bowl about one inch above the pepper on the plate. The

negatively charged spoon will attract the pepper, which not only has a positive electrical charge but also is light enough to be drawn upward to the spoon. (For added visual excitement, stir the pepper together with some salt; its grains, being bigger, will not rise as soon as the pepper, thus separating the seemingly inseparable seasonings.)

SOME NATIONAL FOOD OBSERVANCES: FEBRUARY

Entire month:

	National Cherry Month
	National Grapefruit Month
	National Snack Food Month
1st:	National Baked Alaska Day
2nd:	National Heavenly Hash Day
3rd:	National Carrot Day
	National Carrot Cake Day
4th:	National Stuffed Mushroom Day
5th:	National Chocolate Fondue Day
6th:	National Frozen Yogurt Day
7th:	National Fettuccine Alfredo Day
9th:	National Bagels and Lox Day
10th:	National Cream Cheese Brownie Day
12th:	National Plum Pudding Day
13th:	National Tortini Day (a type of Italian filled pasta)
15th:	National Gum Drop Day
16th:	National Almond Day
17th:	National Café au Lait Day
18th:	National Crab-Stuffed Flounder Day
19th:	National Chocolate Mint Day
20th:	National Cherry Pie Day
21st:	National Sticky Bun Day
21st–27th:	National Pancake Week
22nd:	National Margarita Day
23rd:	National Banana Bread Day
24th:	National Tortilla Chip Day
26th:	National Pistachio Day
27th:	National Kahlua Day
28th:	National Chocolate Soufflé Day
29th:	National Surf and Turf Day

DIETARY LAWS OF DEUTERONOMY

14:3 Thou shalt not eat any abominable thing.

14:4 These *are* the beasts which ye shall eat: the ox, the sheep, and the goat,

14:5 The hart, and the roebuck, and the fallow deer, and the wild goat, and the pygarg, and the wild ox, and the chamois.

14:6 And every beast that parteth the hoof, and cleaveth the cleft into two claws, *and* cheweth the cud among the beasts, that ye shall eat.

14:7 Nevertheless these ye shall not eat of them that chew the cud, or of them that divide the cloven hoof; *as* the camel, and the hare, and the coney: for they chew the cud, but divide not the hoof; *therefore* they *are* unclean unto you.

14:8 And the swine, because it divideth the hoof, yet cheweth not the cud, it *is* unclean unto you: ye shall not eat of their flesh, nor touch their dead carcase.

14:9 These ye shall eat of all that *are* in the waters: all that have fins and scales shall ye eat:

14:10 And whatsoever hath not fins and scales ye may not eat; it *is* unclean unto you.

14:11 *Of* all clean birds ye shall eat.

14:12 But these *are they* of which ye shall not eat: the eagle, and the ossifrage, and the ospray,

14:13 And the glede, and the kite, and the vulture after his kind,

14:14 And every raven after his kind,

14:15 And the owl, and the night hawk, and the cuckoo, and the hawk after his kind,

14:16 The little owl, and the great owl, and the swan,

14:17 And the pelican, and the gier eagle, and the cormorant,

14:18 And the stork, and the heron after her kind, and the lapwing, and the bat.

14:19 And every creeping thing that flieth *is* unclean unto you: they shall not be eaten.

14:20 *But of* all clean fowls ye may eat.

14:21 Ye shall not eat *of* anything that dieth of itself: thou shalt give it unto the stranger that *is* in thy gates, that he may eat it; or thou mayest sell it unto an alien: for thou *art* an holy people unto the LORD thy God.

Thou shalt not seethe a kid in his mother's milk.

—The Holy Bible (King James Version)

ON ROAST MUTTON

Gently stir and blow the fire,
Lay the mutton down to roast,
Dress it quickly, I desire,
In the dripping put a toast,
That I hunger may remove—
Mutton is the meat I love.
On the dresser see it lie;
Oh, the charming white and red;
Finer meat ne'er met the eye,
On the sweetest grass it fed:
Let the jack go swiftly round,
Let me have it nice and brown'd.
On the table spread the cloth,
Let the knives be sharp and clean,
Pickles get and salad both,
Let them each be fresh and green.
With small beer, good ale and wine,
Oh ye gods! how I shall dine.

—Jonathan Swift (1667–1745)

TEA, CAKES, AND MEMORIES

One day in winter, as I came home, my mother, seeing that I was cold, offered me some tea, a thing I did not ordinarily take. I declined at first, and then, for no particular reason, changed my mind. She sent for one of those short, plump little cakes called "petites madeleines," which look as though they had been molded in the fluted scallop of a pilgrim's shell. And soon, mechanically, weary after a dull day with the prospect of a depressing morrow, I raised to my lips a spoonful of the tea in which I had soaked a morsel of the cake. No sooner had the warm liquid, and the crumbs with it, touched my palate, then a shudder ran through my whole body, and I stopped, intent upon the extraordinary changes that were taking place. An exquisite pleasure had invaded my senses, but individual, detached, with no suggestion of its origin. And at once the vicissitudes of life had become indifferent to me, its disasters innocuous, its brevity illusory—this new sensation having had on me the effect which love has of filling me with a precious essence; or rather this essence was not in me, it was myself. I had ceased now to feel mediocre, accidental, mortal. Whence could it have come to me, this all-powerful joy? I was conscious that it was connected with the taste of tea and cake, but that it infinitely transcended those savors, could not, indeed, be of the same nature as theirs. Whence did it come? What did it signify? How could I seize upon and define it?

I drink a second mouthful, in which I find nothing more than in the first, a third, which gives me rather less than the second. It is time to stop; the potion is losing its magic. It is plain that the object of my quest, the truth, lies not in the cup but in myself. The tea has called up in me, but does not itself understand, and can only repeat indefinitely with a gradual loss of strength, the same testimony; which I, too, cannot interpret, though I hope at least to be able to call upon the tea for it again and to find it there presently, intact and at my disposal, for my final enlightenment. I put down my cup and examine my own mind. It is for it to discover the truth.

—*Remembrance of Things Past* (1913–1927), Marcel Proust

THE MIRACLE OF LEFTOVERS

The most remarkable thing about my mother is that for thirty years she served the family nothing but leftovers. The original meal has never been found. —Calvin Trillin (b. 1935)

A FATE FIT FOR A CUCUMBER

It has been a common saying of physicians in England, that a cucumber should be well sliced, and dressed with pepper and vinegar, and then thrown out, as good for nothing.

—Samuel Johnson, quoted in *The Journal of a Tour to the Hebrides* (1785) by James Boswell

RANDOM STATS, PART II: GOURMET FOODS

$20,000: Black market value of a suitcase filled with smuggled caviar.

$100,000: Street value of that suitcase filled with smuggled caviar.

100-plus years: Maximum age of the beluga sturgeon, source of caviar.

2,500 pounds: Maximum weight of the sturgeon.

20: Percent of a mature female sturgeon's weight yielded in caviar.

130,000 pounds: Average annual U.S. imports of caviar, 1989 to 1997.

½ to 1 ounce: Average suggested serving size for caviar.

$6.6 million: Value of that average annual 130,000 pounds of caviar.

95 percent: Amount of world caviar demand centered on the European Union, Switzerland, United States, and Japan.

2 to 3 pounds: Average weight of a goose foie gras.

523: Calories in four ounces of foie gras.

85.47 percent: Calories from fat in foie gras.

4.7 percent: Calories from carbohydrate in foie gras.

3,600 years: Approximate length of time humankind has been searching for and eating truffles.

2 to 15 inches: Depth below ground at which black truffles are found.

4 to 5 feet: Distance from an oak tree's base of an average black truffle.

1,000 metric tonnes: French black truffle production in 1892.

50 to 90 metric tonnes: Current average French truffle production, due to deforestation and environmental changes.

1,000: Approximate number of truffle-hunting dogs in Europe.

$800 to $1,500: Price range per pound for truffles.

10 percent: U.S. vinegar sales in 2002 attributable to balsamic vinegar.

400: Approximate number of oyster species worldwide.

50-plus gallons: Amount of water per day an average healthy three-inch adult oyster can filter.

SOME HEIRLOOM TOMATOES

So-called "heirloom" varieties of tomatoes, with their unusual colors, shapes, patterns, and flavors (not to mention imaginative names), were in danger of becoming forgotten or lost because they did not provide the long keeping properties, resistance to the hustle and bustle of shipping, or consistency and familiarity of product demanded by modern mass merchandising. Now, thanks to enterprising seed and plant companies, enthusiastic home growers, and dedicated small producers who sell through farmer's markets, they are finding their way back to kitchens everywhere. A selection from the hundreds of heirloom varieties:

Abraham Lincoln: Very dark red, smooth-skinned, three-inch-diameter fruit.

Amana Orange: Originated in Iowa's Amana colonies, large and bright orange with sweet, full-bodied taste.

Anna Russian: Heart-shaped pink fruit three inches in diameter, originally brought to Oregon by a Russian immigrant.

Aunt Gertie's Gold: Golden one-pound fruit with excellent flavor.

Aunt Ruby's German Green: Up to one and a half pounds each, lime-green skin with darker stripes, dark-green flesh, and a very sweet, spicy flavor.

Baby Heart: Mild heart-shaped cherry tomatoes.

Banana Legs: Pairs of small, light-orange fruit shaped like little bananas.

Believe It Or Not: Deep-pink, large, juicy, meaty fruit with great flavor.

Big Rainbow: Very large sweet golden fruit streaked with red.

Black Brandywine: From Amish country, oval-shaped, purple-black, and very flavorful.

Bloody Butcher: Blood-red medium-sized round fruit with robust taste.

Box Car Willie: From three-fourths to one pound each, free of cracks, a prolific home producer, with great taste.

Brandywine: As flavorful as its name, with bright red fruit weighing from one to one and a half pounds, big enough to slice for a large burger.

Bulgarian Triumph: Just two inches in diameter, heart shaped, with excellent taste.

Burbank: Orange colored, medium sized, good flavor.

Cherokee Chocolate: As deep reddish-brown as the popular confection, with a good sweet flavor.

Costuloto Genovese: Italian variety with sweet, deep red half-pound fruit.

Cuore de Toro (Bull's Heart): Sweet Italian heart-shaped variety, pink and meaty, weighing up to two pounds each.

Great White: Large juicy white fruit with a yellow blush, few seeds, and a mild, sweet taste.

Green Grape: Bright green, sweet cherry-sized fruit.

Green Zebra: Medium-sized, round, sweet and spicy fruit with green and yellow stripes.

Hawaiian Pineapple: Multi-lobed fruit five inches in diameter with reddish-orange skin and deep pineapple-yellow flesh.

Hillbilly: A West Virginia variety with skin streaked orange, red, and pink.

Mister Stripey: Mild, firm fruit striped red and yellow-orange.

Money Maker: An English variety prolific enough to be a cash crop, with lots of quarter-pound, bright red-orange fruit.

Mortgage Lifter: Meaty pinkish-red fruit up to one pound each, with few seeds.

Nebraska Wedding: Good-sized bright orange round fruit with excellent sweet-and-tangy flavor.

Old Ivory Egg: Sized, shaped, and colored like a hen's egg, with sweet flavor.

Orange Oxheart: Heart-shaped orange fruit up to three-fourths of a pound each.

Pixie Peach: Little yellow fruit with slightly fuzzy skins.

Plum Lemon: Golden fruit with a mild, slightly citrusy flavor.

Prize of the Trail: Small, sweet orange-colored cherry tomatoes.

Sausage: Cylindrical red fruit as long and slender as small sausages, with great flavor.

Tangerine: Orange, flattened spherical shape like their namesake fruit, with a rich, sweet taste.

Taxi Yellow: Bright yellow, medium-sized, and mild.

Watermelon Beefsteak: Fruit as large as two pounds or more, shaped and colored like watermelon flesh.

White Wonder: Small to medium, with ivory-colored flesh.

A TASTE FOR CAVIAR

Under cover of the clinking of water goblets and silverware and bone china, I paved my plate with chicken slices. Then I covered the chicken slices with caviar thickly as if I were spreading peanut butter on a piece of bread. Then I picked up the chicken slices in my fingers one by one, rolled them so the caviar wouldn't ooze off and ate them.

—*The Bell Jar* (1963), Sylvia Plath

HISTORY IN A NUTSHELL

Lord Henry and his lady were the hosts;
The party we have touch'd on were the guests:
Their table was a board to tempt even ghosts
To pass the Styx for more substantial feasts.
I will not dwell upon *ragoûts* or roasts,
Albeit all human history attests
That happiness for man—the hungry sinner!—
Since Eve ate apples, much depends on dinner.
— *Don Juan*, Canto the Thirteenth (1823),
George Gordon, Lord Byron

LESS CONVENTIONAL JELLY BEAN FLAVORS

Jelly Belly brand jelly beans, founded in Los Angeles in 1976, achieved fame as the preferred treat of President Ronald Reagan, who kept a jar of them in the Oval Office and on Air Force One. But in addition to producing such traditional jelly bean flavors as cherry, lemon, lime, grape, orange, and licorice, Jelly Belly has set a new standard in candy creativity. Some of the more creative choices from its list of 50 flavors (see www.jellybelly.com for more information):

+ Bubble Gum
+ Buttered Popcorn
+ Cafe Latte
+ Cantaloupe
+ Cappuccino
+ Caramel Corn
+ Chocolate Pudding
+ Cotton Candy
+ Cream Soda*
+ Green Apple*

+ Jalapeño
+ Margarita
+ Peanut Butter
+ Piña Colada
+ Pink Grapefruit
+ Plum
+ Strawberry Cheesecake
+ Toasted Marshmallow
+ Tangerine*
+ Watermelon

* One of the original eight flavors launched by the company.

CHEAT SHEET I: SOME JAPANESE FOODS

Aemono: Vegetable or seafood salads with a dressing based on *miso*, tofu, or sesame seeds.

Agemono: Fried foods, including *tempura.*

Chawan-mushi: Steamed savory egg custard studded with pieces of shrimp, chicken, shiitake mushroom, spinach, and scallion.

Chirashizuki:. A luncheon box filled with sushi rice topped with sliced raw fish and pickled vegetables.

Donburi: A lunchtime specialty consisting of a bowl of rice topped with all manner of sautéed, fried, pickled, or raw ingredients.

Gohanmono: Rice dishes, including *donburi.*

Miso soup: A thin broth or water enriched with miso paste, made from fermented soybeans, and garnished with cubes of tofu, pieces of seaweed, and chopped scallions.

Ramen: Thin wheat noodles, usually enjoyed in soup.

Sake: Referred to as "rice wine," this thin, clear to pale amber rice-based liquid is actually brewed like beer. Usually served warm.

Sashimi: Very fresh raw fish, sliced.

Shabu-shabu: Very thinly sliced beef or other meats, cooked along with vegetables and noodles at table by swishing them back and forth in simmering water (creating a sound that inspired the dish's name) until cooked, then dipping them in a sauce before eating.

Soba: Buckwheat noodles.

Sukiyaki: Thinly sliced beef cooked with vegetables, tofu, and noodles in a flavorful broth based on soy sauce and rice wine.

Sunomono: Vinegar-seasoned salads, usually served as side dishes or appetizers.

Sushi: *Sashimi* artfully molded together with balls of seasoned rice. (See also "Five Regional Japanese Favorites You Probably Won't Find in Your Local Sushi Bar," page 112.)

Tsukemono: Assorted pickles cured with vinegar, salt, and other seasonings.

Udon: Thick wheat noodles.

Wasabi: A fiery-hot green paste made by reconstituting the dried and powdered root of a type of horseradish, usually mixed with soy sauce as a dip for *sashimi* and *sushi.*

Yakitori: Bite-sized pieces of food seasoned with a sweet, thick soy sauce and grilled on skewers over a charcoal fire.

PAIRING WESTERN WINE WITH FAR EASTERN CUISINE

Wines made from grape juice are foreign to Asia. However, the basic principles of food and wine pairing can lead to some enjoyable choices.

Chinese: Pick a big, spicy wine with good fruit and a hint of sweetness such as a Gewürztraminer or Riesling. Californian or Australian Chardonnays without too much oak are also good. Light, fruity reds such as Beaujolais or Zinfandel go well with chicken or pork.

Indian: Complement Indian cuisine's rich bouquet of spices with aromatic wines that are often described as spicy or fruity. With seafood or poultry, try Pinot Gris, Gewürztraminer, or Riesling, or a sparkling rosé with a hint of sweetness. For more robust chicken, beef, or lamb dishes, select a young Zinfandel, a Californian Syrah, or an Australian Shiraz.

Japanese: This subtle cuisine calls for sparkling wines, "blush" wines, or light Rieslings with an edge of sweetness.

Korean: Robust Korean foods welcome whites such as Chardonnay or Sauvignon Blanc and reds like Pinot Noir, Cabernet Sauvignon, and Merlot.

Thai: Complex, high-profile seasonings such as chilies, lemongrass, and coconut milk welcome spicy Gewürztraminer and crisp Sauvignon Blanc.

Vietnamese: Its subtle seasonings and rare hints of spice go well with lighter whites, including young unoaked Chardonnays and Sauvignon Blancs, as well as lighter reds such as Zinfandels and Merlots.

THE HISTORY OF A SQUASH

Once upon a time a farmer planted a little seed in his garden, and after a while it sprouted and became a vine and bore many squashes. One day in October, when they were ripe, he picked one and took it to market. A gorcerman [sic] bought and put it in his shop. That same morning, a little girl in a brown hat and blue dress, with a round face and snub nose, went and bought it for her mother. She lugged it home, cut it up, and boiled it in the big pot, mashed some of it with salt and butter, for dinner. And to the rest she added a pint of milk, two eggs, four spoons of sugar, nutmeg, and some crackers, put it in a deep dish, and baked it till it was brown and nice, and next day it was eaten by a family named March.

—*Little Women* (1868), Louisa May Alcott

A RECIPE FOR VIRTUE AND CONTENTMENT

How good one feels when one is full—how satisfied with ourselves and with the world! People who have tried it, tell me that a clear conscience makes you very happy and contented; but a full stomach does the business quite as well, and is cheaper, and more easily obtained. One feels so forgiving and generous after a substantial and well-digested meal—so noble-minded, so kindly-hearted.

It is very strange, this domination of our intellect by our digestive organs. We cannot work, we cannot think, unless our stomach wills so. It dictates to us our emotions, our passions. After eggs and bacon, it says, "Work!" After beefsteak and porter, it says, "Sleep!" After a cup of tea (two spoonsful for each cup, and don't let it stand more than three minutes), it says to the brain, "Now, rise, and show your strength. Be eloquent, and deep, and tender; see, with a clear eye, into Nature and into life; spread your white wings of quivering thought, and soar, a god-like spirit, over the whirling world beneath you, up through long lanes of flaming stars to the gates of eternity!"

After hot muffins, it says, "Be dull and soulless, like a beast of the field—a brainless animal, with listless eye, unlit by any ray of fancy, or of hope, or fear, or love, or life." And after brandy, taken in sufficient quantity, it says, "Now, come, fool, grin and tumble, that your fellow-men may laugh—drivel in folly, and splutter in senseless sounds, and show what a helpless ninny is poor man whose wit and will are drowned, like kittens, side by side, in half an inch of alcohol."

We are but the veriest, sorriest slaves of our stomach. Reach not after morality and righteousness, my friends; watch vigilantly your stomach, and diet it with care and judgment. Then virtue and contentment will come and reign within your heart, unsought by any effort of your own; and you will be a good citizen, a loving husband, and a tender father—a noble, pious man. —*Three Men In a Boat* (1889), Jerome K. Jerome

DASHES, PINCHES, SPOONS, AND CUPS

1 dash	=	$\frac{1}{16}$ teaspoon
1 pinch	=	$\frac{1}{8}$ teaspoon
3 teaspoons	=	1 tablespoon
4 tablespoons	=	$\frac{1}{4}$ cup
16 tablespoons	=	1 cup

EATING AND DRINKING ACROSS THE MAP, PART II:
MEAT, POULTRY, AND SEAFOOD DEPARTMENT

Bacon, Idaho
Barbecue, North Carolina
Chicken, Alaska
Clam, Virginia
Fish, Georgia
Ham, England
  (also Quebec, Canada)
Ham Lake, Minnesota
Hamburger Lake, Utah
Lamb, Colorado
Marrowbone, Tennessee
Oyster, Virginia
Oystermouth, Wales
Shrimp Bay, Alaska
Shrimp Bayou, Louisiana

Shrimp Creek, Georgia
Shrimp Hill, Pennsylvania
Shrimp Lagoon, Louisiana
Shrimp Lake, Montana
Squid Bay, Alaska
Squid Cove, Maine
Squid Island, Maine
Steak Creek, Alaska
Steak Lake, Minnesota
Steakhouse Hill, Idaho
Tuna, Pennsylvania
Turkey, Arkansas
Turkey Creek, Western Australia
Turkey Hill, Alabama

RANDOM STATS, PART III: SOFT DRINKS

The following statistics were compiled by the Beverage Marketing
Corporation.

72.1 percent: Coca-Cola company market share in Albania in 2002 (2.99
  gallons consumed per capita).
19.4 percent: Pepsi-Cola company market share in Albania in 2002 (0.81
  gallon consumed per capita).
8.4 percent: All other soft drink companies' market share in Albania in
  2002 (0.35 gallon consumed per capita).
26.3 percent: Flavor share held by cola in Armenia's soft drink market in
  2002 (0.85 gallon consumed per capita).
17.1 percent: Flavor share held by orange in Armenia's soft drink market
  in 2002 (0.55 gallon consumed per capita).
12 percent: Flavor share held by lemon-lime in Armenia's soft drink market in 2002 (0.39 gallon consumed per capita).
44.5 percent: Flavor share held by all other flavors combined in Armenia's
  soft drink market in 2002 (combined 1.43 gallons consumed per capita).

CHEAT SHEET II: SOME CHINESE FOODS

Beggar's chicken: A whole chicken baked in a thick coating of clay, which hardens in the oven and is broken open at serving time.

Bird's nest soup: Subtle, slightly gelatinous soup prepared by simmering the nests of swiftlets—made by the birds from seaweed dissolved with their saliva—in chicken broth.

Char siu: Chinese-style roast pork.

Dim sum: A wide range of bite-sized steamed, baked, or fried savory and sweet treats, served as a morning or midday meal. (See also "Ten Classic Dim Sum Varieties," page 14.)

Fire pot: A main course of bite-sized pieces of meat, poultry, seafood, or vegetables, cooked at table by dipping into simmering broth, then dipped into a sauce and eaten. The resulting rich soup is enjoyed last.

Hot and sour soup: From the Szechuan province, a thick soup of poultry stock, soy sauce, sesame oil, vinegar, hot chili oil, shredded roasted meat, mushrooms, tofu, and bamboo shoots.

Kung pao: Named in honor of an imperial courtier, this stir-fry is based on chicken, beef, or other protein, cooked with chili paste, bean sauce, whole dried red chilies, and whole roasted peanuts.

Mu shu: A stir-fry of shredded pork or other meat or chicken, with scallions, delicate mushrooms, tiger-lily buds, egg, soy sauce, and rice wine, folded into thin soft wheat pancakes with a dab of soy-based sweet-and-salty hoisin sauce.

Peking (or Beijing) duck: Roast crispy-skinned duck, eaten by rolling slices of the rich meat and skin in thin wheat pancakes with sweet-salty hoisin sauce, green onion, and cucumber.

THE DEAN OF AMERICAN CUISINE'S IMAGINARY LAST MEAL

I've long said that if I were about to be executed and were given a choice of my last meal, it would be bacon and eggs. There are few sights that appeal to me more than the streaks of lean and fat in a good side of bacon, or the lovely round of pinkish meat framed in delicate white fat that is Canadian bacon. Nothing is quite as intoxicating as the smell of bacon frying in the morning, save perhaps the smell of coffee brewing.

—James Beard (1903–1985)

SAYING GRACE: SOME TRADITIONAL CHRISTIAN PRAYERS

Thank you for the food we eat,
Thank you for the friends we meet,
Thank you for the birds that sing,
Thank you God for everything.
Amen.

◆

Bless us, O Lord, and these Thy gifts,
Which we are about to receive
From Thy bounty through Christ our Lord.
Amen.

◆

Be present at our table, Lord,
Be here and everywhere adored.
Thy creatures bless and grant that we
May feast in paradise with Thee.
Amen.
—John Wesley (1703–1791)

◆

Gracious giver of all good food,
We thank you for rest and food.
Grant that all we do or say
May serve you humbly today.
Amen.

◆

God is great and God is good,
And we thank him for our food.
By his hand we all are fed.
Give us, Lord, our daily bread.
Amen.

SOME NATIONAL FOOD OBSERVANCES: MARCH

Entire month:

	National Flour Month
	National Frozen Food Month
	National Noodle Month
	National Nutrition Month
	National Peanut Month
	National Sauce Month
2nd:	National Banana Cream Pie Day
3rd:	National Mulled Wine Day
4th:	National Pound Cake Day
6th:	National Frozen Food Day
	National Chocolate Cheesecake Day
7th:	National Crown Roast of Pork Day
8th:	National Peanut Cluster Day
9th:	National Crabmeat Day
10th:	National Blueberry Popover Day
12th:	National Baked Scallops Day
14th:	National Potato Chip Day
15th:	National Pears Helene Day
16th:	National Pasta Day
	National Artichoke Hearts Day
18th:	National Lacy Oatmeal Cookie Day
19th:	National Chocolate Caramel Day
20th:	National Ravioli Day
21st:	National French Bread Day
22nd:	National Bavarian Crepes Day
23rd:	National Chip and Dip Day
24th:	National Chocolate Covered Raisins Day
25th:	National Lobster Newburg Day
28th:	National Black Forest Cake Day
29th:	National Lemon Chiffon Cake Day
30th:	National Hot Dog Day
31st:	National Clams on the Half-Shell Day

POOR RICHARD ON FOOD AND DRINK

American patriot and founding father Benjamin Franklin (1706–1790) shared many observations on the pleasures and foibles of food and drink in his prolific writings, most notably his *Poor Richard: An Almanack*, which he wrote and published annually from 1732 to 1758. (See also "Ben Franklin on How to Make Wine," pages 158–159.)

Eat to live, and not live to eat.

◆

Eat not to dullness. Drink not to elevation.

◆

Three good meals a day is bad living.

◆

Hunger is the best pickle.

◆

To lengthen thy life, lessen thy meals.

◆

I saw few die of hunger; of eating, a hundred thousand.

◆

In general, mankind, since the improvement of cookery,
eats twice as much as nature requires.

◆

The king's cheese is half wasted in parings; but no matter,
'tis made of the people's milk.

◆

We hear of the conversion of water into wine at the marriage
in Cana as of a miracle. But this conversion is, through the goodness
of God, made every day before our eyes. Behold the rain which
descends from heaven upon our vineyards, and which incorporates
itself with the grapes, to be changed into wine; a constant proof
that God loves us, and loves to see us happy.

◆

There cannot be good living where there is not good drinking.

◆

Wine makes daily living easier, less hurried, with fewer
tensions and more tolerance.

◆

He that drinks his Cyder alone, let him catch his Horse alone.

◆

He that drinks fast, pays slow.

◆

Drink does not drown Care, but waters it, and makes it grow faster.

◆

Before Noah, men having only water to drink, could not find the truth.
. . . This good man, Noah, having seen that all his contemporaries had
perished by this unpleasant drink, took a dislike to it; and God, to relieve
his dryness, created the vine and revealed to him the art of making le vin.
By the aid of this liquid he unveiled more and more truth.

◆

Take counsel in wine, but resolve afterwards in water.

◆

Beer is proof that God loves us and wants us to be happy.

HINDU FOOD PRAYERS FROM THE BHAGAVAD GITA

Before a Meal
Brahmaarpanam Brahma Havir
Brahmaagnau Brahmanaa Hutam
Brahmaiva Tena Gantavyam
Brahma Karma Samaadhinaha

—Bhagavad Gita, 4:24

[Any means or act of offering is Brahman (the Ultimate Truth). The fire
in which the offering is made is Brahman. Anyone who makes the offering
is Brahman. Any person who abides or acts in the spirit of Brahman indeed
attains Brahman.]

After a Meal
Aham Vaishvaanaro Bhutva
Praaninaam Dehamaashritha
Praanaapaana Samaa Yuktaha
Pachaamyannam Chatur Vidham

—Bhagavad Gita, 15:14

[I am Vaishnavara, existing as digestive fire in the body of every living
being. United with inhaled *(prana)* and exhaled *(apaana)* life breaths, I
digest all four kinds of food (bitten and chewed; chewed with the tongue;
gulped; swallowed) and I purify them.]

FOOD AND DRINK IN COCKNEY RHYMING SLANG

Reputedly first developed centuries ago as a secret language among the less savory element of working-class Londoners, Cockney rhyming slang endures today as a colorful argot enjoyed by many Britons. New terms still appear, often inspired by celebrities of the day. Not surprisingly, food and, especially, drink appear frequently in the jargon, both in slang terms that sound like food and drink but aren't, and terms that don't but are. Note that slang terms involving multiple words are often abbreviated to the first word. Thus, "Pour me a saga" would be the way someone in a pub might request a lager; or somebody with sore feet might exclaim, "Oh, me achin' plates!"

Doesn't sound like food or drink but is . . .

Slang	Meaning
Acker Bilk	Milk
Army and navy	Gravy
Blind mice	Ice
Cinderella	Stella (Stella Artois beer)
Clothes peg	Egg
Day and night	Light (ale)
Deep sea glider	Cider
Dog's eye	Meat pie
Easy rider	Cider
Edna Everidge	Beverage
Everton toffee	Coffee
Fine and dandy	Brandy
Finger and thumb	Rum
Forsythe Saga	Lager
Gay and frisky	Whisky
Gary Glitter	Bitter (ale)
Giorgio Armani	Sarnie (sandwich)
Gold watch	Scotch
Half past three	Tea
Harvey Nichols	Pickles
Inspector Morse	Sauce
Isle of Skye	Pie
Jack the Dandy	Brandy
Jack the Ripper	Kipper

Slang	Meaning
Jay-Z	Cup of tea
Jockey's whips	Chips (French fries)
John Cleese	Cheese
Kate and Sydney	Steak and kidney (pie)
Kiki Dee	Tea
Knobbly knees	Peas
Lillian Gish	Fish
Loop the loop	Soup
Mahatma Gandhi	Brandy
Mick Jagger	Lager
Mickey Rourke	Pork
Mutter and stutter	Butter
Needle and pin	Gin
Nose and chin	Gin
Penelope Cruz	Booze
Pinky and perky	Turkey
Philharmonic	Gin and tonic
Pimple and blotch	Scotch
Plink plonk	Vin blanc (white wine)
Pocket watch	Scotch
Porcupine	Wine
Pull down the shutter	Butter
Sexton Blake	Cake
Stand at ease	Cheese
Stop thief	Beef
Supersonic	Tonic
Talk and mutter	Butter
Ten furlongs (mile and a quarter)	Water
Tiddly wink	Drink
Tom Cruise	Booze
Tom Thumb	Rum
Uncle Reg	Veg (vegetables)
Uri Geller	Stella (Stella Artois beer)
Twist and shouts	Sprouts (Brussels)
Vera Lynn	Gin
Waterloo	Stew
Winona Ryder	Cider
You and me	Tea

Sounds like food or drink but isn't . . .

Slang	Meaning
Apple core	Score (£20 note)
Apples and pears	Stairs
Bacon and eggs	Legs
Bacon rind	Blind
Bag (or bowl) of fruit	Suit
Baked beans	Jeans
Baked potato	See you later
Bangers and mash	Cash
Bath bun	Son
Biscuit and cookie	Bookie or rookie
Biscuits and cheese	Knees
Bottle of Scotch	Watch
Bread and butter	Gutter
Bread and cheese	Sneeze
Bread and honey	Money
Brown bread	Dead
Brussels sprout	Shout or scout
Cadbury Snack	Back
Chicken and rice	Nice
Chicken curry	Worry
Chocolate fudge	Judge
Cocoa	Say so
Cooking fat	Cat
Corn on the cob	Job
Cornish pasty	Nasty
Crust of bread	Head
Currant bun	Nun, son, or sun
Custard and jelly	Telly (TV)
Eggs and kippers	Slippers
Fish and tater	Later
Fruit and nuts	Guts
Ginger ale	Jail
Gooseberry puddin'	Woman (wife)
Green eggs and ham	Exam
Ham and cheesy	Easy

Slang	Meaning
Ham and eggs	Legs
Ham shanks	Yanks (Americans)
Hot potato	Waiter
Ice cream freezer	Geezer
Irish stew	True
Jam roll	Dole (welfare)
Jam tart	Heart
Lager and lime	Time
Lemon curd	Bird (woman) or word
Loaf of bread`	Head
Lollipop	Shop
Mince pies	Eyes
Orange and pear	Swear
Peas in the pot	Hot
Pie and mash	Crash
Pineapple	Chapel
Pineapple chunk	Bunk (bed)
Plates of meat	Feet
Pork pies	Lies
Quaker Oat	Coat
Rhubarb crumble	Grumble
Roast pork	Fork
Rum and coke	Joke
Sausage roll	Dole (welfare) or goal
Spanish onion	Bunion
Sugar candy	Handy
Tea leaf	Thief
Wobbly jelly	Telly (TV)

Sounds like food or drink and is . . .

Slang	Meaning
Apple fritter	Bitter (ale)
Cockles and mussels	Brussels (sprouts)
Pig's ear	Beer
Salmon and trout	Stout (beer)
Sticky toffee	Coffee

CHEAT SHEET III: SOME GREEK, TURKISH, MIDDLE EASTERN, AND NORTH AFRICAN FOODS

Avgolemono: Rich tangy Greek chicken soup or sauce made with egg *(avgo)* and lemon *(lemono).*

Baba ghanoush: Literally "harem girl," a voluptuous puree of roasted eggplant, garlic, lemon, and tahini (sesame-seed paste), served as an appetizer.

Baklava: Pastry composed of tissue-thin sheets of phyllo dough, layered with chopped nuts, butter, and sweet spices; baked; soaked in honey syrup; and then cut into diamond-shaped pieces.

Börek: A baked turnover made from paper-thin sheets of phyllo dough, folded or rolled around a savory filling of lamb, beef, goat cheese, or vegetables, or a sweet filling of nuts or cheese.

Couscous: Tiny, grainlike pasta, usually served with a fragrant meat, poultry, or vegetable stew.

Dolmades: Grape leaves rolled around rice or another savory filling.

Falafel: A mixture of pureed chickpeas, cracked wheat, garlic, cumin, and other seasonings, formed into balls or little patties and deep-fried to be served as a snack or stuffed inside the natural pocket of pita bread to make a sandwich.

Ful medammes: Egyptian favorite of boiled dried broad beans mashed with olive oil, lemon juice, and garlic, garnished with chopped egg.

Keftedes: Greek meatballs, made from ground beef mixed with bread crumbs, onion, fresh herbs, and egg, fried in olive oil.

Kibbeh: Lebanese specialty of raw lamb pounded with cracked wheat, onion, mint, olive oil, and spices.

Köfte: Similar to *keftedes,* a Turkish favorite usually formed into patty shapes and charcoal-grilled.

Méchoui: Algerian whole spit-roasted lamb.

Moussaka: Greek casserole of eggplant, ground lamb, tomato sauce, and an egg-enriched cheese sauce.

Pastitsio: Greek casserole of macaroni, ground beef or lamb, tomatoes, onions, oregano, and a touch of cinnamon.

Spanakopita: Spinach, feta cheese, and egg encased in flaky phyllo pastry.

Tabbouleh: A Lebanese salad of steamed cracked wheat, chopped tomatoes, onions, scallions, mint, parsley, olive oil, and lemon juice.

Taramasalata: A Greek dip of carp roe blended with bread crumbs, olive oil, lemon juice, onion, and garlic.

Tzatziki: Greek dip of yogurt, garlic, and shredded cucumber.

SOME MILESTONES IN FOOD AND DRINK HISTORY:
1ST TO 12TH CENTURIES AD

14: In Rome, Marcus Gavius Apicius publishes *De Re Coquinaria* (Regarding Cooking), the first true cookbook, including recipes for fish stew, lamb stew, roast whole pig, stuffed dormouse, roast and braised crane, and eggs with honey.

33: Jesus of Nazareth joins with his 12 apostles to hold a Jewish Passover seder, which becomes his Last Supper.

406: Invading Vandals, Sciri, and Alans introduce butter to olive-oil-eating Romans.

629: The body of Islamic laws called Shariah sets forth the rules by which Muslims must eat and prepare their food, including proscription from eating pork, ape, dog, cat, and carnivores.

708: In China, tea begins to take hold as a popular beverage.

805: Tea is introduced to Japan.

850: Coffee, so legend has it, is discovered in Ethiopia.

1066: Norman Conquest of England introduces the words *boeuf* (beef), *veau* (veal), *mouton* (mutton), *porc* (pork), and *poularde* (poultry) to the English language.

1070: Roquefort cheese reportedly discovered in France.

A ROLLICKING TEATIME!

Now to the banquet we press;
Now for the eggs, the ham,
Now for the mustard and cress,
Now for the strawberry jam!
Now for the tea of our host,
Now for the rollicking bun,
Now for the muffin and toast,
Now for the gay Sally Lunn!*
—*The Sorcerer* (1877), W. S. Gilbert

* A rich English egg-and-butter bread, served at teatime, reputedly named either for a baker in Bath, England, or corrupted from the French *sol et lune*, "sun and moon," describing both the round shape and golden color.

FUN WITH FOOD & DRINK, PART II:
HOW TO SLICE A BANANA WITHOUT PEELING IT

It may seem impossible, but a touch of ingenuity helps create a real surprise for the unsuspecting banana-eater.

1. **Pick the right banana.** Start with a ripe banana that has a generous speckling of brown spots on the skin, which will camouflage your subterfuge.
2. **Prepare needle and thread.** Thread a sewing needle with a double strand about eight inches long of clean white thread, knotted at the end as you would prepare it for sewing on a button.
3. **Insert the needle.** About one-third of an inch from one end of the banana—at a point where there is a brown spot along one of the ridges of the peel—insert the needle perpendicular to the banana's length, passing it under the peel and along the circumference of the fruit inside, then out at the next ridge, preferably through another spot.
4. **Reinsert the needle.** Then reinsert the needle at the exact spot from which it emerged, continuing to pass it under the peel to the next ridge and out through another spot.
5. **Encircle the fruit.** Repeat until the needle comes out of the first hole into which you inserted it. The thread will now be encircling the fruit, just beneath the peel. Grasp the knotted and needle ends of the thread firmly between your thumb and forefinger, holding both digits up against the starting/ending hole. With your other hand, pull both ends, thus slicing the fruit with the encircling thread.
6. **Repeat the process.** Repeat at intervals of one-third of an inch all along the length of the banana.
7. **Replace the banana.** Put the whole unpeeled banana in a bowl at the breakfast table, ready to surprise the first person who peels it.

METRIC CONVERSIONS: FLUID OUNCES, CUPS, QUARTS, AND GALLONS
TO MILLILITERS AND LITERS, AND VICE VERSA

The metric system defines a liter (commonly abbreviated as "l") as the volume occupied by one cubic decimeter of water. To use metric cookbooks with American cooking tools, or vice versa, liters and milliliters (ml, that is, one thousandth of a liter) must be converted to the old imperial measurement system of fluid ounces (fl oz), cups (c, equivalent to 8 ounces), pints (pts, equivalent to 2 cups), quarts (qts, equivalent to 2 pints or 4 cups), and gallons (gals, equivalent to 4 quarts, 8 pints, or 16 cups). A pair of formulas you can easily perform with a calculator make it possible to do conversions.

To convert milliliters to fluid ounces, use the following formula:
$$ml \times .034 = fl\ oz$$

To convert fluid ounces to milliliters, use the following formula:
$$fl\ oz \div .034 = ml$$

For ease, use the following chart instead of performing calculations. Note that metric equivalents are uniformly rounded to make measuring liquid volumes slightly less painstaking. [Note, too, that British ounces are slightly smaller than American ounces, with 1 U.S. ounce equal to 1.04 United Kingdom (U.K.) ounces. U.S. ounces are used in the following chart. Take this into account when trying to cook from an old pre-metric British cookbook.]

fl oz/c/pt/qt/gal	ml/l	fl oz/c/pt/qt/gal	ml/l
2 fl oz (¼c)	60 ml	1¾ c	430 ml
3 fl oz (⅓c)	90 ml	2 c (1 pt)	500 ml
4 fl oz (½c)	125 ml	2½ c	625 ml
5 fl oz (⅔c)	160 ml	3 c	750 ml
6 fl oz (¾c)	180 ml	3½ c	875 ml
1 c	250 ml	4 c (1 qt)	1 l
1¼c	310 ml	8 c (2 qts)	2 l
1½ c	375 ml	1 gal (4 qts)	4 l

A FINE KITCHEN

Some sensible person once remarked that you spend the whole of your life either in your bed or your shoes. Having done the best you can by shoes and bed, devote all the time and resources at your disposal to the building up of a fine kitchen. It will be, as it should be, the most comforting and comfortable room in the house.   —Elizabeth David (1913–1992)

MARK TWAIN'S HOMECOMING "LITTLE BILL OF FARE"

In *A Tramp Abroad* (1880), faced with European hotel fare he found appalling, Mark Twain drew up a "little bill of fare" he imagined for his homecoming meal in America:

Radishes. Baked apples, with cream.	Oysters roasted in shell-Northern style.
Fried oysters; stewed oysters. Frogs.	
American coffee, with real cream.	Soft-shell crabs. Connecticut shad.
American butter.	Baltimore perch.
Fried chicken, Southern style.	Brook trout, from Sierra Nevadas.
Porter-house steak.	Lake trout, from Tahoe.
Saratoga potatoes.	Sheep-head and croakers, from New Orleans.
Broiled chicken, American style.	
Hot biscuits, Southern style.	Black bass from the Mississippi.
Hot wheat-bread, Southern style.	American roast beef.
Hot buckwheat cakes.	Roast turkey, Thanksgiving style.
American toast. Clear maple syrup.	Cranberry sauce. Celery.
Virginia bacon, broiled.	Roast wild turkey. Woodcock.
Blue-points, on the half shell.	Canvas-back-duck, from Baltimore.
Cherry-stone clams.	Prairie hens, from Illinois.
San Francisco mussels, steamed.	Missouri partridges, broiled.
Oyster soup. Clam soup.	Possum. Coon.
Philadelphia Terapin soup.	Boston bacon and beans.

Bacon and greens, Southern style.	Green corn, on the ear.
Hominy. Boiled onions. Turnips.	Hot corn-pone with chitlings, Southern style.
Pumpkin. Squash. Asparagus.	
Butter bean. Sweet potatoes.	Hot hoe-cake, Southern style.
Lettuce. Succotash. String beans.	Hot egg-bread, Southern style.
Mashed potatoes. Catsup.	Hot light-bread, Southern style.
Boiled potatoes, in their skins.	Buttermilk. Iced sweet milk.
New potatoes, minus the skins.	Apple dumplings, with real cream.
Early rose potatoes, roasted in the ashes, Southern style.	Apple pie. Apple Fritters.
	Apple puffs, Southern style.
Sliced tomatoes, with sugar or vinegar. Stewed tomatoes.	Peach cobbler, Southern style.
	Peach pie. American mince pie.
Green corn, cut from the ear and served with butter and pepper.	Pumpkin pie. Squash pie.
	All sorts of American pastry.

Fresh American fruits of all sorts, including strawberries which are not to be doled out as if they were jewelry, but in a more liberal way.
Ice-water—not prepared in the ineffectual goblet, but in the sincere and capable refrigerator.

SOME NATIONAL FOOD OBSERVANCES: APRIL

Entire month:

	National Florida Tomato Month
	National Food Month
	National Soy Foods Month
1st:	National Sourdough Bread Day
2nd:	National Peanut Butter and Jelly Day
3rd:	National Chocolate Mousse Day
5th:	National Raisin and Spice Bar Day
6th:	National Caramel Popcorn Day
7th:	National Coffee Cake Day
9th:	National Chinese Almond Cookie Day
10th:	National Cinnamon Crescent Day
11th:	National Cheese Fondue Day
12th:	National Licorice Day
12th–18th:	National Egg Salad Week
13th:	National Peach Cobbler Day
14th:	National Pecan Day
15th:	National Glazed Ham Day
16th:	National Eggs Benedict Day
17th:	National Cheeseball Day
18th:	National Animal Crackers Day
19th:	National Garlic Day
20th:	National Pineapple Upside-Down Cake Day
21st:	National Chocolate-Covered Cashews Day
22nd:	National Jelly Bean Day
23rd:	National Cherry Cheesecake Day
24th:	National Pigs-in-a-Blanket Day
25th:	National Zucchini Bread Day
26th:	National Pretzel Day
27th:	National Prime Rib Day
28th:	National Cracker Day
	National Blueberry Pie Day
29th:	National Shrimp Scampi Day
30th:	National Oatmeal Cookie Day

A SONG OF ONE'S OWN SOUP

'Oh, a song, please, if the Mock Turtle would be so kind,' Alice replied, so eagerly that the Gryphon said, in a rather offended tone, 'Hm! No accounting for tastes! Sing her "Turtle Soup," will you, old fellow?'

The Mock Turtle sighed deeply, and began, in a voice sometimes choked with sobs, to sing this:—

'Beautiful Soup, so rich and green,
Waiting in a hot tureen!
Who for such dainties would not stoop?
Soup of the evening, beautiful Soup!
Soup of the evening, beautiful Soup!
Beau—ootiful Soo—oop!
Beau—ootiful Soo—oop!
Soo—oop of the e—e—evening,
Beautiful, beautiful Soup!

'Beautiful Soup! Who cares for fish,
Game, or any other dish?
Who would not give all else for two
Pennyworth only of beautiful Soup?
Pennyworth only of beautiful Soup?
Beau—ootiful Soo—oop!
Beau—ootiful Soo—oop!
Soo—oop of the e—e—evening,
Beautiful, beauti—FUL *soup!*'

—*Alice's Adventures in Wonderland* (1865), Lewis Carroll

AN INNOCENT'S VIEW OF MIDDLE EASTERN COFFEE

Of all the unchristian beverages that ever passed my lips, Turkish coffee is the worst. The cup is small, it is smeared with grounds; the coffee is black, thick, unsavory of smell, and execrable in taste. The bottom of the cup has a muddy sediment in it half an inch deep. This goes down your throat, and portions of it lodge by the way, and produce a tickling aggravation that keeps you barking and coughing for an hour.

—*The Innocents Abroad* (1869), Mark Twain

CHEAT SHEET IV:
SOME MEXICAN, LATIN AMERICAN, AND CARIBBEAN FOODS

Anticuchos: Peruvian snack or appetizer of skewered and grilled chunks of spicy marinated beef heart.

Blaff: Firm-fleshed white fish quickly poached with wine, water, allspice, chilies, cloves, garlic, lime slices, scallions, and whole peppercorns.

Callaloo: A soup from the Antilles, based on sharp-tasting leaves of the callaloo plant, okra, onions, garlic, cloves, spices, chicken broth, and coconut milk.

Chilaquiles: Stale corn tortillas cut into strips, lightly fried, and baked with chili sauce and other ingredients such as cheese or meat.

Chimichurri: A traditional Argentine condiment, served with steak and other grilled foods, combining oil, garlic, parsley, oregano, and chili flakes.

Empanada: Baked or fried turnover filled with a range of well-seasoned savory mixtures.

Enchilada: Literally "chillied," a corn tortilla rolled around a savory filling and baked with a chili sauce.

Feijoada: Brazil's festive stew of well-seasoned black beans accompanied by cured and fresh meats, sausages, greens, rice, chili-lime sauce, and oranges.

Flauta: Corn tortilla rolled around a filling into a flute shape, then deep-fried.

Guacamole: Pureed avocado mixed with lime juice and such other embellishments as chopped onion, tomato, and cilantro.

Matambre: A "hunger killer" Argentine appetizer of thin steak stuffed and rolled with spinach, carrots, eggs, onions, peppers, bacon, garlic, and other embellishments, cooked, cooled, and sliced to reveal a colorful spiral pattern.

Mole: One of many thick, savory sauces from central Mexico, and dishes featuring them, the best known of which include bitter chocolate.

Patty: Turnover with a spicy meat filling.

Pibil: From Mexico's Yucatan Peninsula, a traditional Mayan dish of chicken or other meat marinated with citrus juice, garlic, herbs, spices, and annatto seeds (which give a bright red color), then wrapped in banana leaves and baked until tender.

Quesadilla: A flour or corn tortilla filled with mild cheese and then cooked on a griddle or deep-fried until crisp.

Relleno: "Stuffed," usually referring to a large roasted mild poblano chili pepper filled with cheese, dipped in batter, and deep-fried.

Seviche: Appetizer of raw seafood marinated with chilies and herbs in citrus juice, whose acidity turns it firm and opaque, as if cooked.

Tamale: Common to Mexico and other Central American and Caribbean countries, a steamed dumpling of cornmeal with a savory or sweet filling, wrapped in cornhusks, a banana leaf, or some other natural wrapper.

SOME BASIC TABLE MANNERS

Attend my words, my gentle knave,
And you shall learn from me
How boys at dinner may behave
With due propriety.

Guard well your hands: two things have been
Unfitly used by some;
The trencher for a tambourine,
The table for a drum.

We could not lead a pleasant life,
And 'twould be finished soon,
If peas were eaten with the knife,
And gravy with the spoon.

Eat slowly: only men in rags
And gluttons old in sin
Mistake themselves for carpet bags
And tumble victuals in.

*　　*　　*

Think highly of the Cat: and yet
You need not therefore think
That portly strangers like your pet
To share their meat and drink.

The end of dinner comes ere long
When, once more full and free,
You cheerfully may bide the gong
That calls you to your tea.

—"Stans Puer ad Mensam" (1923), Walter Alexander Raleigh

CONFUCIUS (551–479 BC) ON FOOD AND DRINK

A superior man, even for the space of a single meal,
will not act contrary to humanity.

◆

Everyone eats and drinks, but few appreciate taste.

◆

How you cut your meat reflects how you live your life.

◆

It is hard to deal with one who stuffs himself with food all day,
without applying his mind to anything good.

◆

Only the drinking of wine should not be unlimited,
but not to the point of confusion.

◆

The honorable and upright man keeps well away from both the
slaughterhouse and the kitchen and allows no knives on his table.

◆

The man of virtue, in eating, does not seek satiety.

◆

The object of the superior man is truth, not food.

◆

With coarse rice to eat, water to drink, and my bended arm
for a pillow: Even in these may I find joy.

EATING AND DRINKING ACROSS THE MAP, PART III:
WINE, BEER, AND LIQUOR DEPARTMENT

Alcohol Creek, Minnesota (also Wisconsin)
Beer, England
Beer Bottle Crossing, Idaho
Bourbon, Illinois (also Indiana, Kentucky, Mississippi, and Missouri)
Brandy, Pennsylvania
Corkscrew, Florida
Gin City, Arkansas
Martini Creek, California
Martini Run, Kentucky
Rum Branch, Missouri
Stout, California (also Iowa, Mississippi, Ohio, Tennessee, and Texas)
Tequila Cove, Nevada
Whiskey Bend, Washington

Whiskey Dick, Oregon

Whiskey Ford, Texas

Whiskey Hill, Oregon

Whiskey Springs, California

Whiskeytown, California

Whisky Falls, California

Whiskyville, Ohio

Wine Hill, Illinois

Winedale, Texas

SEED COUNTS

Have you ever stared at an ear of corn and wondered how many kernels it has, or regarded a strawberry and gone cross-eyed considering all those tiny black seeds on its surface? Wonder no more. Here are the approximate number of seeds you will find in these foods.

Fruit or Vegetable	Seed Count
Apple	5
Avocado	1
Blackberry	80
Corn	800
Fava bean pod	6–8
Orange	20–56
Orange, Mandarin	6
Orange, "seedless" navel	0–6
Pomegranate	800
Pumpkin	500
Strawberry	200
Tangerine	15
Tomato	100
Watermelon	140
Watermelon, "seedless"	6

A WORTHY SUBJECT FOR DISCUSSION

Do not be afraid to talk about food. Food which is worth eating is worth discussing. And there is the occult power of words which somehow will develop its qualities.

—*Simple French Cooking for English Homes* (1923), X. Marcel Boulestin

"SMOKING CHOWDER" FOR EVERY MEAL

Upon making known our desires for a supper and a bed, Mrs. Hussey, postponing further scolding for the present, ushered us into a little room, and seating us at a table spread with the relics of a recently concluded repast, turned round to us and said – "Clam or Cod?"

"What's that about Cods, ma'am?" said I, with much politeness.

"Clam or Cod?" she repeated.

"A clam for supper? a cold clam; is that what you mean, Mrs. Hussey?" says I; "but that's a rather cold and clammy reception in the winter time, ain't it, Mrs. Hussey?"

But being in a great hurry to resume scolding the man in the purple shirt, who was waiting for it in the entry, and seeming to hear nothing but the word "clam," Mrs. Hussey hurried towards an open door leading to the kitchen, and bawling out "clam for two," disappeared.

"Queequeg," said I, "do you think that we can make out a supper for us both on one clam?"

However, a warm savory steam from the kitchen served to belie the apparently cheerless prospect before us. But when that smoking chowder came in, the mystery was delightfully explained. Oh, sweet friends! hearken to me. It was made of small juicy clams, scarcely bigger than hazel nuts, mixed with pounded ship biscuit, and salted pork cut up into little flakes; the whole enriched with butter, and plentifully seasoned with pepper and salt. Our appetites being sharpened by the frosty voyage, and in particular, Queequeg seeing his favorite fishing food before him, and the chowder being surpassingly excellent, we despatched it with great expedition: when leaning back a moment and bethinking me of Mrs. Hussey's clam and cod announcement, I thought I would try a little experiment. Stepping to the kitchen door, I uttered the word "cod" with great emphasis, and resumed my seat. In a few moments the savory steam came forth again, but with a different flavor, and in good time a fine cod-chowder was placed before us.

We resumed business; and while plying our spoons in the bowl, thinks I to myself, I wonder now if this here has any effect on the head? What's that stultifying saying about chowder-headed people? "But look, Queequeg, ain't that a live eel in your bowl? Where's your harpoon?"

Fishiest of all fishy places was the Try Pots, which well deserved its name; for the pots there were always boiling chowders. Chowder for breakfast, and chowder for dinner, and chowder for supper, till you began to look for fish-bones coming through your clothes. The area before the house was paved with clam-shells. Mrs. Hussey wore a polished necklace of codfish vertebra; and Hosea Hussey had his account books bound in superior old shark-skin. There was a fishy flavor to the milk, too, which I could not at all account for, till one morning happening to take a stroll along the beach among some fishermen's boats, I saw Hosea's brindled cow feeding on fish remnants, and marching along the sand with each foot in a cod's decapitated head, looking very slip-shod, I assure ye.

—*Moby Dick* (1851), Herman Melville

FORBIDDEN FOODS

The following proscribed foods should not be served to guests of the following ethnic or religious backgrounds.

Africans (certain tribes): Fish.
Eskimos (certain tribes): Mixed ocean and land ingredients.
Ethiopian Christians: Camel.
Hindus: Beef.
Jews: Pork, shellfish, mixed milk and meat products.
Melanesians: Stingray, bush pig.
Mongolians: Duck.
Mormons: Alcohol, coffee, tea.
Moslems: Pork, shellfish.
Omaha Indians (Wind Clan): Shellfish.
Ponapeans (Caroline Islands, South Pacific): Turtles, immature plants or animals.

MIND YOUR OWN BELLY

Some people have a foolish way of not minding, or pretending not to mind, what they eat. For my part, I mind my belly very studiously and very carefully, for I look upon it that he who does not mind his belly will hardly mind anything else.

—Samuel Johnson, quoted in *The Life of Samuel Johnson* (1791)
by James Boswell

ABRAHAM LINCOLN'S FIRST INAUGURAL LUNCHEON

Served on Monday, March 4, 1861.

Mock Turtle Soup[*]

◆

Corned Beef and Cabbage

◆

Parsley Potatoes

◆

Blackberry Pie

◆

Coffee

*A rich broth of oxtail, standing in for more costly sea turtle meat, seasoned with tomatoes, onion, lemon, allspice, and cloves, then garnished with sherry and chopped hard-boiled egg.

RANDOM STATS, PART IV: FROZEN FOOD

$26.6 billion: U.S. retail volume of frozen food sales in 2001.

$25.07 billion: U.S. retail volume of frozen food sales in 2000.

$5.9 billion: Approximate current annual retail volume of frozen dinners and entrees in the United States.

£4.983 billion: U.K. retail volume of frozen food sales in 1999, according to a study conducted by Unilever Ice Cream and Frozen Food.

£218.26 million: U.K. retail volume in 1999 spent on heat-and-serve frozen traditional British-style meals, according to the same source.

£303.96 million: U.K. retail volume in 1999 spent on heat-and-serve frozen international-style meals, according to the same source.

96 percent: U.S. owners of table-service restaurants who say they use frozen foods, according to the National Restaurant Association.

76 percent: U.S. restaurant owners who believe technological advances in the coming decade will make prepared frozen foods indistinguishable from fresh.

94 percent: U.S. shoppers who say they sometimes buy frozen food on an average supermarket visit, according to a poll conducted by Tupperware.

30 percent: U.S. shoppers who say they always buy frozen food.

ON DRESSING AND COOKING A TROUT

Take your trout, wash, and dry him with a clean napkin; then open him, and having taken out his guts, and all the blood, wipe him very clean within, but wash him not; and give him three scotches with a knife to the bone, on one side only. After which take a clean kettle, and put in as much hard stale beer, (but it must not be dead) vinegar, and a little white wine, and water, as will cover the fish you intend to boil: then throw into the liquor a good quantity of salt, the rind of a lemon, a handful of sliced horse-radish-root, with a handsome little fagot of rosemary, thyme, and winter-savory. Then set your kettle upon a quick fire of wood, and let your liquor boil up to the height before you put in your fish: and then, if there be many, put them in one by one, that they may not so cool the liquor, as to make it fall. And whilst your fish is boiling, beat up the butter for your sauce with a ladle-full or two of the liquor it is boiling in. And, being boiled enough, immediately pour the liquor from the fish: and, being laid in a dish, pour your butter upon it; and, strewing it plentifully over with shaved horse-radish, and a little pounded ginger; garnish your sides for your dish, and the fish itself with a sliced lemon or two, and serve it up.

—*The Compleat Angler, Part II* (1676), Charles Cotton (*Note:* Cotton wrote the sequel to the English fly-fishing classic penned by his more celebrated friend and mentor, Izaak Walton.)

GAUGING DONENESS BY HAND

Before the advent of instant-read thermometers, chefs tested the doneness of meats—particularly steaks and chops—by hand. The process is simple: With an index finger, quickly but firmly press down on the thickest part of the meat, taking care to keep your hands and arms well clear of the heat source. Then, compare the "give" in the meat to the way your palm and wrist feel when pressed in the same way, using the chart below (see also "Doneness Temperatures," page 79). (Thanks to my friend Wolfgang Puck for demonstrating to me this method.)

Doneness	Feels Like . . .
Rare	Fleshy part just below the thumb
Medium	Base of palm closer to the wrist
Well-done	Top of wrist, just below the palm

EDIBLE FIGURES OF SPEECH: SAVORY

- Bring home the *bacon*.
- A hill of *beans*.
- *Beef* it up.
- Have a *beef* with someone.
- Know which side your *bread* is *buttered* on.
- *Butter* wouldn't melt in his/her mouth.
- *Chicken* out.
- *Clam* up.
- Make a lot of *dough*.
- A lot of *fish* in the sea.
- *Fritter* away.
- Everything else is just *gravy*.
- Riding the *gravy* train.
- *Grill* the suspect.
- *Ham* it up.
- Use your *noodle*.
- Can't make an *omelet* without breaking *eggs*.
- Go *nuts*.
- *Salad* days.
- *Salt* of the earth.
- Take it with a grain of *salt*.
- Worth his/her *salt*.
- *Pork barrel* politics/legislation.
- Couch *potato*.
- Hot *potato*.
- Not my cup of *tea*.
- Can't get blood from a *turnip*.
- Hot *tomato*.
- *Veg* out.

TICKLING THE GULLET

Hot mockturtle vapour and steam of newbaked jampuffs rolypoly poured out from Harrison's. The heavy noonreek tickled the top of Mr. Bloom's gullet. Want to make good pastry, butter, best flour, Demerara sugar, or they'd taste it with the hot tea.   —*Ulysses* (1922), James Joyce

EDIBLE FIGURES OF SPEECH: SWEET

- *Apple* of my eye.
- American as *apple pie.*
- Slip on a *banana* peel.
- It's a piece of *cake.*
- That takes the *cake.*
- Life is a bowl of *cherries.*
- Life is like a box of *chocolates.**
- One tough *cookie.*
- That's the way the *cookie* crumbles.
- They're the *crème de la crème.*
- The upper *crust.*
- Crazy as a *fruitcake.*
- *Fudge* the data.
- Like *honey* to a bee.
- The *icing on the cake.*
- That car is a *lemon.*
- As slow as *molasses.*
- *Peachy* keen.
- Easy as *pie.*
- *Plum* perfect.
- As wrinkled as a *prune.*
- The proof is in the *pudding.***
- Pour on the *sugar.*
- Plain *vanilla.*

* The phrase was probably coined and definitely popularized by the character portrayed by Tom Hanks in the movie *Forrest Gump* (1994).

** The popular usage given here is actually a corruption of the full and correct saying, "The proof of the pudding is in the eating."

BRING ON THE BACON AND EGGS

Bring porridge, bring sausage, bring fish for a start,
Bring kidneys and mushrooms and partridges' legs,
But let the foundation be bacon and eggs.
—A. P. Herbert (1890–1971)

SOME PASTA SHAPES

Most, but not all, pasta names come from Italy and are accurate, or sometimes fanciful, descriptions of the shapes. In general, choose more delicate strands such as capellini (angel hair) or spaghettini to go with lighter sauces, broader strands or ribbons such as fettuccine to go with heavier sauces, bite-sized shapes with indentations such as shells or radiatore to go with chunky sauces, and large tubes or shells for stuffing and baking.

Acini di pepe: "Peppercorns," tiny bead shapes for soup.
Agnolotti: "Fat lambs," bite-sized stuffed pasta similar to *ravioli.*
Alphabets: Small, letter-shaped noodles, usually served in soups.
Anelli: "Little rings" for soup.
Angel hair: See *cappelli d'angelo.*
Bow ties: See *farfalle.*
Bucatini: "Little holes," resembling hollow strands of thick *spaghetti.*
Cannelloni: "Large pipes," big tubes for stuffing and baking.
Capelli d'angelo *or* **capellini:** "Angel hair," long, thin strands.
Cappelletti: "Little hats," bite-sized filled conical shapes.
Conchiglie: "Shells," shaped like conches, from small bite-sized to large ones for stuffing.
Creste di galli: "Rooster's comb," a bite-sized ruffled and curved shape.
Ditalini: "Little thimbles," small fingertip-sized tubes.
Elicoidali: "Helixes" in the form of straight tubes covered in ridges curving around them at an angle.
Farfalle: "Butterflies," small to bite-sized shapes resembling bow ties.
Fettuccine: "Small ribbons," long, flat strands about one-quarter inch wide.
Fiori: "Flowers," resembling small blossoms or snowflakes.
Funghini: "Small mushrooms," resembling tiny mushrooms, usually for soup.
Fusilli: "Fuses," like long corkscrewed strands of *spaghetti.*
Gemelli: "Twins," two strands about three inches long, twisted together.
Gigli: "Lilies," bite-sized slender ruffled flower shapes.
Gnocchi: "Lumps" of thumbprint-shaped pasta slightly resembling the familiar dumplings of the same name.
Lasagne: Based on a Latin word for pot, broad ribbons with fluted edges.
Linguine: "Little tongues," resembling slightly flattened strands of *spaghetti.*

Lumache: "Snails," resembling small curved shells.

Macaroni: "Dumplings," small curved tubes also known as "elbows."

Maccheroni alla ghitarra: "Homemade guitar pasta," resembling *spaghetti* strands that are square rather than circular in cross-section, cut from rolled-out sheets of dough with a multi-stringed cutter.

Maltagliati: "Badly cut," scraplike shapes of flattened pasta.

Manicotti: "Little muffs," ridged tubes for stuffing and baking.

Millerighe: "Thousand ridges," large bite-sized tubes covered in many fine ridges.

Mostaccioli: "Little moustaches," another name for *penne*.

Occhi di lupo: "Wolf's eyes," thick tubes about one and a half inches long.

Occhi di pernice: "Bird's eyes," small ring shapes.

Orecchiette: "Ears," resembling small, curved cuplike shapes.

Orzo: "Barley," resembling plump grains of rice.

Paglia e fieno: "Straw and hay," *fettuccine* made from batches of yellow egg dough and green spinach dough.

Pastina: "Little doughs," tiny shapes for soup, usually in the form of stars.

Pansotti: "Little bellies," triangular stuffed pastas.

Penne: "Quill pens," slender tubes with ends cut at an angle.

Perciatelle: "Pierced," strands similar to *bucatini*.

Radiatore: "Radiators," bite-sized shapes with multiple parallel wavy ridges.

Ravioli: "Wraps," bite-sized stuffed pasta.

Rigatoni: "Grooved" tubes.

Riso: "Rice," slightly smaller than *orzo*.

Rotelle: "Little wheels," actually resembling corkscrews.

Rotini: "Twists," twisted ribbons in bite-sized lengths.

Ruote: "Wagon wheels," bite-sized shapes resembling wheels with spokes.

Semi de melone: "Melon seeds," shaped and sized exactly like their name.

Spaghetti: "String" or "cord," long slender strands.

Stelle: "Stars," small for soups.

Strozzapreti: "Priest stranglers," long bite-sized ribbons curled up lengthwise and slightly curved.

Tagliatelle: "Little cuts," ribbons slightly narrower than *fettuccine*.

Tortellini: "Little cakes," bite-sized stuffed shapes.

Tubettini: "Little tubes," about one-fourth inch in length.

Vermicelli: "Little worms," more slender than *spaghetti* but more robust than *capelli d'angelo*.

Ziti: "Bridegrooms," slightly curved slender tubes of medium length.

SOME NATIONAL FOOD OBSERVANCES: MAY

Entire month:
National Asparagus Month
National Barbecue Month
National Egg Month
National Hamburger Month
National Salad Month
National Strawberry Month
1st: National Chocolate Parfait Day
1st–7th: National Raisin Week
2nd: National Truffles Day
3rd: National Raspberry Popover Day
4th: National Candied Orange Peel Day
5th: National Chocolate Custard Day
National Hoagie Day
6th: National No Diet Day
National Crepes Suzette Day
7th: National Roast Leg of Lamb Day
8th: National Coconut Cream Pie Day
9th: National Butterscotch Brownie Day
10th: National Shrimp Day
11th: National Mocha Torte Day
12th: National Nutty Fudge Day
13th: National Apple Pie Day
14th: National Buttermilk Biscuit Day
15th: National Chocolate Chip Day
16th: National Cherry Cobbler Day
18th: National Cheese Souffle Day
19th: National Devil's Food Cake Day
20th: National Quiche Lorraine Day
21st: National Strawberries 'n' Cream Day
National Wait Staff (Waitresses and Waiters) Day
22nd: National Vanilla Pudding Day
23rd: National Taffy Day
24th: National Escargot Day
26th: National Blueberry Cheesecake Day

27th:	National Grape Popsicle Day
28th:	National Hamburger Day
30th:	National Mint Julep Day
31st:	National Macaroon Day

FOURTEEN CLASSIC WINE-TASTING TERMS

A few of the many words wine experts use:

Acidity: A sharp, lively, refreshing quality resulting from a grape's natural acids.

Appley: Reminiscent in flavor of apples, due to malic acid. This flavor is common in young Chardonnays and less expensive sparkling wines.

Balance: The relative relationship of various flavor elements, including *acidity, fruit, tannin,* and *oakiness.*

Berrylike: Evoking ripe, juicy fruit flavors such as blackberries and raspberries.

Body: A wine's feeling of weightiness in the mouth, resulting from its *tannins,* alcohol level, and concentration of *fruit.*

Bouquet: The aroma, especially when it has grown more complex with bottle-aging.

Complex: Having many different flavor elements.

Earthy: Evoking, through aroma and flavor, the clean scent of freshly tilled, damp soil.

Finish: The way in which a wine's flavor lingers in the mouth. Wines that linger a while are said to have a "long finish."

Flowery: Having an aroma that evokes flowers. The term is generally applied to lighter white wines.

Fruit: The noticeable presence of good fruit flavors, whether of the actual grapes from which the wine was made or reminiscent of other juicy fruits such as berries, apples, cherries, or plums.

Nose: Another term for a wine's aroma.

Oakiness: The presence of oak flavor, derived from the barrel in which a wine is aged.

Tannin: A substance present both in grapes and in new oak barrels, which contributes a harsh edge that, in the proper proportion, adds balance to wines, especially reds.

ON THE ORIGINS OF ROASTING?

The swine-herd, Ho-ti, having gone out into the woods one morning, as his manner was, to collect mast for his hogs, left his cottage in the care of his eldest son Bo-bo, a great lubberly boy, who being fond of playing with fire, as younkers of his age commonly are, let some sparks escape into a bundle of straw, which kindling quickly, spread the conflagration over every part of their poor mansion, till it was reduced to ashes. Together with the cottage (a sorry antediluvian make-shift of a building, you may think it), what was of much more importance, a fine litter of new-farrowed pigs, no less than nine in number, perished. China pigs have been esteemed a luxury all over the east from the remotest periods that we read of. Bo-bo was in the utmost consternation, as you may think, not so much for the sake of the tenement, which his father and he could easily build up again with a few dry branches, and the labour of an hour or two, at any time, as for the loss of the pigs. While he was thinking what he should say to his father, and wringing his hands over the smoking remnants of one of those untimely sufferers, an odour assailed his nostrils, unlike any scent which he had before experienced. What could it proceed from?—not from the burnt cottage—he had smelt that smell before—indeed this was by no means the first accident of the kind which had occurred through the negligence of this unlucky young fire-brand. Much less did it resemble that of any known herb, weed, or flower. A premonitory moistening at the same time overflowed his nether lip. He knew not what to think. He next stooped down to feel the pig, if there were any signs of life in it. He burnt his fingers, and to cool them he applied them in his booby fashion to his mouth. Some of the crums of the scorched skin had come away with his fingers, and for the first time in his life (in the world's life indeed, for before him no man had known it) he tasted—crackling! Again he felt and fumbled at the pig. It did not burn him so much now, still he licked his fingers from a sort of habit. The truth at length broke into his slow understanding, that it was the pig that smelt so, and the pig that tasted so delicious; and, surrendering himself up to the new-born pleasure, he fell to tearing up whole handfuls of the scorched skin with the flesh next it, and was cramming it down his throat in his beastly fashion, when his sire entered amid the smoking rafters, armed with retributory cudgel, and finding how affairs stood, began to rain blows upon the young rogue's shoulders, as thick as hail-stones, which Bo-bo heeded not any more than if they had been flies. The tickling pleasure, which he experienced in his lower regions, had rendered him quite callous to any inconveniences he might feel in those remote quarters. His father might lay on but he could not beat him from his pig, till he had fairly made an end of it, when, becoming a little more sensible of his situation, something like the following dialogue ensued.

"You graceless whelp, what have you got there devouring? Is it not enough that you have burnt me down three houses with your dog's tricks, and be hanged to you, but you must be eating fire, and I know not what—what have you got there, I say?"

"O father, the pig, the pig, do come and taste how nice the burnt pig eats."

—"A Dissertation upon Roast Pig" from *Essays of Elia* (1823), Charles Lamb

CINCINNATI CHILI

One sniff or taste of the chili dished up at the approximately two hundred chili parlors in Cincinnati, Ohio—typified by well-known chains such as Skyline, Empress, Gold Star, and Dixie—demonstrates that this particular version of the thick ground-meat stew owes as much to Greek culture as it does to the Southwest. In addition to chili powder, Cincinnati chili is aromatic with seasonings more often found together in Hellenic cooking: cinnamon, nutmeg, and bay leaves, along with vinegar. A touch of cocoa powder often bolsters the sweetness as well.

Also particular to Cincinnati chili, which dates back to Greek immigrants to the city in the 1920s, is the way it is served and the nomenclature for the various options:

+ **One-Way:** A plain bowl of chili.
+ **Two-Way:** Ladled over spaghetti.
+ **Three-Way:** Over spaghetti, topped with shredded Cheddar cheese.
+ **Four-Way:** Over spaghetti, with Cheddar and chopped onion.
+ **Five-Way:** Over spaghetti , with Cheddar, onion, and kidney beans.

Oyster crackers are served alongside as a garnish, whichever way Cincinnati chili is ordered.

One other popular variation is to ladle chili over a hot dog in a bun to make a "Coney" (a nod to the hot dog's association with New York's Coney Island amusement park). Coneys may be further elaborated, most popularly as a "cheese Coney" with mustard, onion, and Cheddar.

FOOD AND DRINK ON FILM

Some movies (available on DVD or VHS) in which eating and drinking play major roles:

Tom Jones (1963): Albert Finney plays the rollicking title character, Susannah York his true love, in this adaptation of the Henry Fielding novel set in early 18th century England, complete with incredibly over-the-top eating scenes.

> *"It is not true that drink alters a man's character. It may reveal it more fully."*
> —From the screenplay by John Osborne

Willy Wonka and the Chocolate Factory (1971): Gene Wilder brings the fabled chocolate factory owner to life in this musical adaptation of Roald Dahl's beloved children's novel.

> *"Inside this room, all of my dreams become realities, and some of my realities become dreams. And almost everything you'll see is eatable, edible—I mean, you can eat almost everything."* —From the screenplay by Roald Dahl

La Grande Bouffe (1973): Not for the faint of heart, this French film features top European stars Marcello Mastroianni, Ugo Tognazzi, Michel Piccoli, and Philippe Noiret as four well-to-do friends who decide to eat themselves to death, along with other indulgences.

Who Is Killing the Great Chefs of Europe? (1978): George Segal and Jacqueline Bisset solve the title mystery in a romantic comedy based on the novel *Someone Is Killing the Great Chefs of Europe* by Nan and Ivan Lyons.

Diner (1982): Steve Guttenberg, Daniel Stern, Mickey Rourke, Kevin Bacon, Timothy Daly, and Paul Reiser come of age in a 1950s Baltimore diner in this classic from director Barry Levinson.

Moonstruck (1987): Italian-American widow Cher falls irresistibly in love with one-handed baker Nicolas Cage.

> *"They say bread is life. So I bake bread, bread, bread. And the years go by! By, by! And I sweat and shovel this stinking dough in and outta this hot hole in the wall."*
> —From the screenplay by John Patrick Shanley

Tampopo (1987): In this offbeat, wide-ranging, contemporary Japanese look at the pleasures of food, Nobuko Miyamoto is a sweet widow who runs a struggling Tokyo noodle shop and is mentored by a ramen-loving truck driver.

Babette's Feast (1988): In this adaptation of a story by Isak Dinesen, French maid Stéphane Audran comes into a fortune and decides to part company with the two stern Danish sisters who employ her by cooking them a spectacular last supper.

Mystic Pizza (1988): A family-run pizzeria in Mystic, Connecticut, is the swirling focal point for the love stories of sisters played by Annabeth Gish, Lili Taylor, and Julia Roberts.

> *"Do you think we'll get that pizza served while it's still hot?"*
> —From the screenplay/story by Amy Holden Jones, Peter Howze,
> Randy Howze, and Alfred Uhry

Red Sorghum (1989): Chinese director Zhang Yimou weaves a spellbinding, sometimes violent and tragic, tale of the growth of a young woman, Gong Li, in 1930s China, from betrothal to a much-older winemaker, to achieving true love.

The Butcher's Wife (1991): Married to a humdrum butcher in Brooklyn, Demi Moore dreams of a more romantic life, and finds it with psychiatrist Jeff Daniels.

Life Is Sweet (1991): In a story improvised by its cast—including Jim Broadbent and Alison Steadman—and director Mike Leigh, much of the action spins around a chaotic restaurant run by Timothy Spall.

Fried Green Tomatoes (1991): Kathy Bates, Jessica Tandy, Mary Stuart Masterson, and Mary Louise Parker bring to life author Fannie Flagg's charming, offbeat tale of friendship, love, and southern cooking.

> *"Secret's in the sauce . . . or so I've been told."*
> —From the screenplay by Fannie Flagg and Carol Sobieski

Dim Sum: Little Bit of Heart (1992): A Chinese American family experiences everyday life, and food, in 1980s San Francisco.

Like Water for Chocolate (1993): An enchanting screen adaptation brings to life Mexican author Laura Esquivel's magical, passionate novel about the links between love and food.

The Wedding Banquet (1993): Acclaimed director Ang Lee explores the nature of love in modern-day society, as set against the elaborate preparations for a grand traditional Chinese wedding banquet.

Eat Drink Man Woman (1994): This comedy/drama revolves around the lives and loves of a present-day master chef in Taipei and his three unmarried daughters.

The Scent of Green Papaya (1994): Life in 1950s Saigon is seen through the eyes of a young servant, whose work preparing a privileged family's meals is shown in lyrical detail.

A Walk in the Clouds (1995): World War II veteran Keanu Reeves searches for love and fulfillment in a magical romance set in California's Napa Valley amidst a multigenerational winemaking family.

Big Night (1996): Stanley Tucci, codirector with Campbell Scott, stars as the ambitious co-owner with brother/chef Tony Shalhoub of an Italian restaurant in New Jersey, planning to throw a grand banquet for an anticipated visit by jazz legend Louis Prima.

> *"Sometimes, spaghetti just likes to be alone."*
> —From the screenplay by Joseph Tropiano and Stanley Tucci

God of Cookery (1996): This hilarious Hong Kong action movie, complete with martial arts, features a famous chef, Stephen Chow, who falls disastrously down on his luck.

Soul Food (1997): Vanessa L. Williams and Vivica A. Fox star in a comedy/drama about the lives of an African American family, centered on the Sunday dinner table.

Dinner Rush (2000): Danny Aiello, owner of a popular New York Italian restaurant, struggles with his chef/son for control of the restaurant, while a favorite sous-chef gets mixed up with the mob.

> *"When did eating become a Broadway production?"*
> —From the screenplay by Brian Katala and Rick Shaughnessy

What's Cooking? (2000): Thanksgiving dinner is hilariously, and touchingly, viewed through the eyes of four different Los Angeles families—Asian, Hispanic, African American, and Jewish.

Woman on Top (2000): A passionate Brazilian chef, Penélope Cruz, heads for San Francisco in search of success in a sensuous, mystical story.

Chocolat (2001): Chocolatier Juliette Binoche shakes up a provincial 1950s French town when she sets up shop and transforms the lives of residents, including Lena Olin, Johnny Depp, Judi Dench, Alfred Molina, and Carrie-Anne Moss.

> *"The first Comte de Reynaud expelled all the radical Huguenots in this village. You and your truffles present a far lesser challenge."*
> —From the screenplay by Robert Nelson Jacobs,
> from the novel by Joanne Harris

Mostly Martha (2001): Martha, an independent, controlled, and attractive young German *nouvelle*-style chef, copes with her sister's death and her grieving niece while falling for an irresistible Italian chef.

The Price of Milk (2001): New Zealand's countryside is the setting for this sweet, fairy-tale romance about a young couple who run a dairy farm.

Tortilla Soup (2001): Hector Elizondo stars as a widower chef and father of three unmarried daughters in this Mexican American resetting of *Eat Drink Man Woman* (see above).

> *"I love toppings. I've always loved toppings. Sometimes I go to restaurants and I just ask for toppings. You know, I say, the more toppings the merrier."*
> —From the screenplay by Vera Blasi, Ramon Menendez, and Tom Musca,
> based on the *Eat Drink Man Woman* screenplay by Hui-Wing Lang and Ang Lee

SOME EDIBLE FLOWERS

Old-fashioned, country-style cooking and modern cutting-edge cuisine share some common ground in the use of edible flowers as garnishes to add hints of aromatic flavor and vivid color to both savory and sweet dishes. Whenever using edible flowers such as those listed below, make absolutely certain that they are safe to eat. Use only the flower specified, double-checking that it is precisely the type of flower listed, and use only the petals, avoiding other parts of the blossom or its plant. Furthermore, buy the flowers only from culinary sources that can certify they were grown without a trace of pesticides; or grow them yourself under the same scrupulous conditions.

Borage: Blue star-shaped blossoms from the herb of the same name have a refreshing taste reminiscent of cucumber. Great with soups, salads, sorbets, or cold beverages.

Calendula: Saffron-colored marigold flowers have a spicy-bitter taste. Use them with salads, soups, pastas, or pilafs.

Carnation: In varying hues, the petals of these popular flowers make delightfully sweet decorations for cakes and other desserts.

Dandelion: Use only sweet-tasting very-young blossoms to garnish salads or hot or cold rice dishes.

Geranium: A wide variety of scented flowers have tastes corresponding to the particular type.

Hibiscus: The citrusy flavor is reminiscent of cranberries. Often steeped in tea.

Jasmine: Very fragrant white flowers are a favorite when mixed with Chinese green tea.

Lavender: Beautiful, highly aromatic purple blooms with an intensely sweet, slightly citrusy taste are used in both savory and sweet dishes.

Linden: Tiny white or yellow flowers taste like honey.

Nasturtium: Yellow to brilliant orange blossoms with a wonderful peppery taste are used with salads, cheeses, sandwiches, and other savory dishes.

Pansy: Colorful little blossoms with a mildly sweet, slightly grassy taste are used with salads, soups, or desserts.

Rose: Blossoms in varying colors have a sweet and fragrant, yet subtle, scent and taste. Popular in salads and desserts.

Violet: Very fragrant, sweet petals are used in desserts or cold drinks.

SOME MILESTONES IN FOOD AND DRINK HISTORY:
12TH TO 15TH CENTURIES AD

1110: In Paris, King Louis VI allows fishmongers to set up stalls outside his palace walls, thus giving birth to the famed Les Halles marketplace.

1123: London's Smithfield meat market is established.

1148: Following the Second Crusade, knights bring sugar back to Europe from the Middle East.

1204: Damson plum trees from Syria are planted in France by knights back from the Fourth Crusade.

1212: Chinese tofu is introduced in Japan.

1265: London's Covent Garden produce market is established.

1274–1292: On his journeys in Asia, mostly under service to Kublai Khan, Italian Marco Polo observes steak tartare, exotic fruits and vegetables, exotic spices, and Asian cooking techniques, knowledge of which he will bring home to Venice.

1319: Sugar is first imported into England.

1380: French royal chef Guillaume Tirel, a.k.a. Taillevent (ca. 1310–1395), publishes the first book on his nation's cuisine, *Le Viander de Taillevent* (roughly, Taillevent's Pantry), including recipes for sauces and stews.

1383: The Löwenbräu brewery is founded in Munich.

1421: Milan, Italy, establishes an official pasta price list.

1430: Valdespine, Spain's oldest sherry producer, is founded in Jerez de la Frontera.

1475: Kiva Han, the first recorded coffeehouse in the world, opens in Constantinople.

1492–1502: Christopher Columbus's ocean journeys to the New World lead to the introduction of such foods as peppers, corn, pineapples, sweet potatoes, and allspice to the Old World, while introducing wheat to the New World.

1498–1499: Sailing for Portugal, Vasco da Gama opens trade routes to India and the Spice Islands.

A WELL-SEASONED LINEAGE

Salt is born of the purest of parents: the sun and the sea.

—Pythagoras (569–475 BC)

SOME NATIONAL FOOD OBSERVANCES: JUNE

Entire month:

    National Candy Month
    National Dairy Month
    National Fresh Fruit and Vegetable Month
    National Ice Tea Month
    National Papaya Month
    National Soul Food Month

1st:	National Doughnut Day
2nd:	National Rocky Road Day
4th:	National Frozen Yogurt Day
5th:	National Gingerbread Day
	National Hunger Awareness Day
6th:	National Applesauce Cake Day
7th:	National Chocolate Ice Cream Day
8th:	National Jelly-Filled Doughnut Day
12th:	National Taco Day
	National Peanut Butter Cookie Day
13th:	National Lobster Day
18th:	National Splurge Day
22nd:	National Chocolate Éclair Day
26th:	National Chocolate Pudding Day
28th:	National Tapioca Day

COFFEE AS LITERARY INSPIRATION

This coffee plunges into the stomach, and immediately there is overall commotion. The mind is aroused, and ideas pour forth like the battalions of the Grande Armée on the field of battle, and the fight begins. Memories charge at full gallop, their banners flying in the wind. The light cavalry of comparisons deploys itself magnificently; the artillery of logic hurry in with their train of ammunition; flashes of wit pop up like sharpshooters. Similes arise and the paper covers with ink: for the struggle commences and concludes with torrents of black liquid, just as a battle with powder.

—*Treatise on Modern Stimulants* (1839), Honoré de Balzac

EATING AND DRINKING ACROSS THE MAP, PART IV:
PANTRY DEPARTMENT

Bean, England
Bean City, Florida
Flourtown, Pennsylvania
Molasses Junction, Florida
Noodle, Texas
Oatmeal, Texas
Pickle Branch, Texas
Pickle Butte, Idaho
Pickle Creek, Arkansas (also Illinois, Kansas, Minnesota, Missouri, Oklahoma, Oregon, and Texas)

Rice, California (also Alabama, Illinois, Kansas, Minnesota, Texas, Virginia, and Washington)
Sauerkraut Creek, Montana
Sauerkraut Hill, Pennsylvania
Sauerkraut Lakes, Wyoming
Sauerkraut Peak, California
Sauerkraut Run, West Virginia
Syrup Branch, Florida
Syrup Lake, Michigan
Wheat Common, England

VEGETARIAN GRAZING

Flopsy, Mopsy, and Cotton-
tail, who were good little
bunnies, went down the lane
to gather blackberries:

But Peter, who was very
naughty, ran straight to Mr.
McGregor's garden, and
squeezed under the gate!

First he ate some lettuces and
some French beans; and then
he ate some radishes;

And then, feeling rather sick, he
went to look for some parsley.

But round the end of a
cucumber frame, whom should
he meet but Mr. McGregor!
—*The Tale of Peter Rabbit* (1902), Beatrix Potter

TASTES LIKE . . .

It's an easy old fallback to say that exotic meats "taste like chicken." The truth is far more complex, as Joe Staton of the Museum of Comparative Zoology at Harvard University revealed in an article entitled "Tastes Like Chicken?" in the July/August 1998 issue of the *Annals of Improbable Research*. Staton summarized his findings in a scientific chart, drastically simplified and summarized below, that divided exotic meats into six different general taste categories. He even made the imaginative leap of including one long-extinct animal by extrapolating findings from similar living species, and another very-much-thriving species based purely on anecdotal evidence.

Beef Taste
+ Cow
+ Buffalo
+ Deer
+ Horse
+ Muskrat
+ Ostrich

Chicken Taste
+ Alligator
+ Chicken
+ Frog
+ Goose
+ Iguana
+ Kangaroo
+ Quail
+ Pigeon
+ Rabbit
+ Salamander
+ Snake
+ Turtle
+ Tyrannosaurus rex

Pork Taste
+ Human
+ Pig

A SALAD-LOVER'S SONG OF PRAISE

Oh, herbaceous treat!
'Twould tempt the dying anchorite to eat;
Back to the world he'd turn his fleeting soul,
And plunge his fingers in the salad bowl;
Serenely full the epicure would say,
"Fate cannot harm me,—I have dined to-day."
—*A Receipt for a Salad*, Sydney Smith (1771–1845)

DONENESS TEMPERATURES

Food-borne bacteria die at a minimum temperature of 160°F. Many people prefer red meat cooked less done, however, which usually presents minimal risk. (Individuals with illnesses affecting the immune system, pregnant women, young children, and the elderly should eat fully cooked meats.) Gauge doneness by inserting an instant-read thermometer into the center of the thickest part of the food, not touching bone. If the meat is done, remove it from the heat and let it rest, covered with foil, for 10 minutes; the temperature will continue to rise slightly from residual heat, while the juices settle back into the meat. (See also "Gauging Doneness by Hand," page 61.)

Food		Temperature
Beef	Rare	120–130°F
	Medium-rare	130–140°F
	Medium	140–150°F
	Medium-well	150–160°F
	Well-done	160–165°F
Chicken	Breast	150–160°F
	Dark meat	165–175°F
Lamb	Rare	125°F
	Medium-rare	130°F
	Medium	140°F
	Medium-well	150°F
	Well-done	160°F
Pork		160°F
Turkey	Breast	150–160°F
	Dark meat	165–175°F
Veal	Medium	145–155°F

JEWISH BARUCHAS (BLESSINGS)

Blessing over Apples and Honey at Rosh Hashanah

Recited before these foods are eaten at a family meal celebrating the Jewish New Year, to ensure a sweet and fruitful year to come:

> Baruch atah Adonai, Elohaynu, melech ha-olam,
> borei p'ri ha-eitz. (Amein.)
> [Blessed art Thou, oh Lord our God, King of the Universe,
> who creates the fruit of the tree. (Amen.)]

Recited immediately after the first bite of apples and honey:

> Y'hee ratzon mee-l'fanecha, Adonai Elohaynu v'elohey avoteynu
> sh'tichadeish aleinu shanah tovah um'tuqah. (Amein.)
> [May it be Your will, oh Lord our God and God of our ancestors,
> that you renew for us a good and sweet year. (Amen.)]

Blessing over Bread

Recited before eating bread immediately following a Sabbath service, or before a meal:

> Baruch atah Adonai, Elohaynu, melech ha-olam,
> ha-motzi lechem min ha-aretz. (Amein.)
> [Blessed art Thou, oh Lord, our God, King of the Universe,
> who brings forth bread from the earth. (Amen.)]

Blessing over Wine

Recited before drinking wine immediately following the blessing over bread, after a Sabbath service or before a meal:

> Baruch atah Adonai, Elohaynu, melech ha-olam,
> borei p'ri ha-gafen. (Amein.)
> [Blessed art Thou, oh Lord our God, King of the Universe,
> who creates the fruit of the vine. (Amen.)]

HIGH-ALTITUDE COOKING AND CANNING

The higher the altitude above sea level at which you cook, the lower the atmospheric pressure will be, and the lower the boiling point of water will be. Many recipes have to be adjusted accordingly when cooking at high altitudes. (Note, however, that cookbooks specifically developed for high altitudes also exist.)

Adjusting ingredients: Depending on altitude, add 2 to 4 extra tablespoons for every 1 cup (250 ml) of liquid.

Baking: Above 3,000 feet (914 meters), use 25 percent less leavening agents. Beat egg whites to softer rather than firmer peaks. For sponge cakes and other delicate baked goods, use 1 extra whole egg. Use 1 to 2 fewer tablespoons of sugar for each 1 cup (250 ml) called for.

Boiling pasta and beans: Increase the quantity of water by 30 to 50 percent.

Canning and preserving: Increase the sterilizing time or pressure depending on the altitude, following guidelines in books or Web sites devoted to preserving.

Deep-frying: Decrease oil temperature by 3°F (1.7°C) for each 1,000 feet (300 meters) above sea level.

Stewing and braising: Add 1 hour to cooking time starting at 4,000 feet (1,200 meters) above sea level, with 1 hour more for each 1,000 feet (300 meters). Add liquid as necessary to keep cooking vessels from boiling dry (see above).

Boiling Point of Water

Altitude in Feet/Meters	Fahrenheit	Celsius
Sea level	212°F	100°C
1,000 feet/305 meters	210°F	98.9°C
2,000 feet/610 meters	208°F	97.8°C
3,000 feet/914 meters	206°F	96.7°C
4,000 feet/1,219 meters	204°F	95.6°C
5,000 feet/1,524 meters	202°F	94.4°C
6,000 feet/1,829 meters	201°F	93.9°C
7,000 feet/2,134 meters	199°F	92.8°C
7,500 feet/2,286 meters	198°F	92.2°C
10,000 feet/3,048 meters	195°F	90.6°C
15,000 feet/4,572 meters	185°F	85.0°C

LAST LUNCH ON THE RMS TITANIC, APRIL 14, 1912

Consommé Fermier[1] Cockie Leekie[2]
Fillets of Brill
Eggs à l'Argenteuil[3]
Chicken à la Maryland[4]
Corned Beef, Vegetables, Dumplings

◆

From the Grill
Grilled Mutton Chops
Mashed, Fried and Baked Jacket Potatoes
Custard Pudding   Apple Meringue   Pastry

◆

Buffet
Salmon Mayonnaise   Potted Shrimps[5]
Norwegian Anchovies   Soused Herrings[6]
Plain & Smoked Sardines
Roast Beef   Round of Spiced Beef
Veal and Ham Pie
Virginia and Cumberland Ham
Bologna Sausage   Brawn
Galantine of Chicken[7]   Corned Ox Tongue
Lettuce   Beetroot   Tomatoes

◆

Cheese
Cheshire, Stilton, Gorgonzola, Edam,
Camembert, Roquefort, St. Ives, Cheddar

◆

Iced draught Munich Lager Beer 3d. & 6d. a Tankard

1. Farmer's-style clear broth garnished with fresh vegetables.
2. Traditional Scottish soup of chicken and leeks, also known as cock-a-leekie.
3. Hard-boiled eggs served in a tartlet shell with asparagus and hollandaise sauce.
4. Usually refers to fried chicken served with cream gravy.
5. Tiny bay shrimps served cold, surrounded by seasoned butter.
6. Fresh raw herring fillets lightly pickled in malt vinegar with spices.
7. Chicken fillets stuffed with ground veal or other meat, then poached, chilled, and sliced.

MIGRAINE TRIGGERS

Medical researchers have found that certain foods and drinks can trigger a migraine headache attack. (Sufferers should keep a diary of episodes and what they ate beforehand, scan the list, and review suspects with a doctor.) Possible culprits:

Alcohol
Aspartame (artificial sweetener)
Avocados
Bananas (especially when overripe)
Beans
Beer
Buttermilk
Caffeinated beverages (coffee, tea, some sodas)
Cheeses (especially aged or moldy varieties)
Chocolate
Chocolate milk
Citrus fruit
Cocoa
Coconut
Coconut oil
Figs
Garlic (especially raw)
Liver
Milk
Monosodium glutamate (a seaweed extract used to enhance flavor in some processed foods and Asian cuisine)
Nuts
Olive oil
Olives
Onions
Papayas
Pickled fish
Pickled meat
Plums, red
Pumpkin seeds
Raisins
Red wine
Salt
Sauerkraut
Sausages preserved with nitrates (such as hot dogs and salamis)
Sesame seeds
Sherry
Smoked fish
Smoked meat
Snow peas
Sour cream
String beans
Sunflower seeds
Tomatoes
Yeast-leavened breads, cakes, and pastries
Yogurt

METRIC CONVERSIONS:
OUNCES AND POUNDS TO GRAMS AND KILOGRAMS

Enthusiastic cooks accustomed to the old imperial measurement system sometimes encounter recipes using metric measurements. In the metric system, 1 gram is defined as the weight in a vacuum of 1 cubic centimeter of pure water at maximum density, and is equivalent to 0.0353 ounce in the imperial measurement system used in the United States. And 1000 grams equals 1 kilogram (kg), which is equivalent to 2.20625 pounds (lb).

To convert ounces (oz) to grams (g), use the following formula:
$$oz \times 28.35 = g$$

To convert grams (g) to ounces (oz), use the following formula:
$$g \div 28.35 = oz$$

Divide ounce amounts larger than 16 by 16 to get weight in pounds (16 ounces = 1 pound).

For ease, and to yield consistent results when converting recipes, refer to the following chart, in which the measurements are rounded.

oz (lb)	g/kg	oz (lb)	g/kg
¼ oz	7 g	12 oz (¾ lb)	375 g
⅓ oz	10 g	13 oz	410 g
½ oz	15 g	14 oz	440 g
¾ oz	20 g	15 oz	470 g
1 oz	30 g	16 oz (1 lb)	500 g
1½ oz	45 g	1¼ lbs	625 g
2 oz	60 g	1½ lbs	750 g
2½ oz	75 g	2 lbs	1 kg
3 oz	90 g	2½ lbs	1.25 kg
3½ oz	105 g	3 lbs	1.5 kg
4 oz (¼ lb)	125 g	3½ lbs	1.75 kg
5 oz (⅓ lb)	155 g	4 lbs	2 kg
6 oz	185 g	5 lbs	2.5 kg
7 oz	220 g	6 lbs	3 kg
8 oz (½ lb)	250 g	7 lbs	3.5 kg
9 oz	280 g	8 lbs	4 kg
10 oz	315 g	9 lbs	4.5 kg
11 oz	345 g	10 lbs	5 kg

A TASTE OF THE FINE LIFE

Emma on entering, felt herself wrapped round by the warm air, a blending of the perfume of flowers and of the fine linen, of the fumes of the viands, and the odour of the truffles. The silver dish covers reflected the lighted wax candles in the candelabra, the cut crystal covered with light steam reflected from one to the other pale rays; bouquets were placed in a row the whole length of the table; and in the large-bordered plates each napkin, arranged after the fashion of a bishop's mitre, held between its two gaping folds a small oval shaped roll. The red claws of lobsters hung over the dishes; rich fruit in open baskets was piled up on moss; there were quails in their plumage; smoke was rising; and in silk stockings, knee-breeches, white cravat, and frilled shirt, the steward, grave as a judge, offering ready carved dishes between the shoulders of the guests, with a touch of the spoon gave you the piece chosen. On the large stove of porcelain inlaid with copper baguettes the statue of a woman, draped to the chin, gazed motionless on the room full of life.

Madame Bovary noticed that many ladies had not put their gloves in their glasses.

But at the upper end of the table, alone amongst all these women, bent over his full plate, and his napkin tied round his neck like a child, an old man sat eating, letting drops of gravy drip from his mouth. His eyes were bloodshot, and he wore a little queue tied with black ribbon. He was the Marquis's father-in-law, the old Duke de Laverdiere, once on a time favourite of the Count d'Artois, in the days of the Vaudreuil hunting-parties at the Marquis de Conflans', and had been, it was said, the lover of Queen Marie Antoinette, between Monsieur de Coigny and Monsieur de Lauzun. He had lived a life of noisy debauch, full of duels, bets, elopements; he had squandered his fortune and frightened all his family. A servant behind his chair named aloud to him in his ear the dishes that he pointed to stammering, and constantly Emma's eyes turned involuntarily to this old man with hanging lips, as to something extraordinary. He had lived at court and slept in the bed of queens! Iced champagne was poured out. Emma shivered all over as she felt it cold in her mouth. She had never seen pomegranates nor tasted pineapples. The powdered sugar even seemed to her whiter and finer than elsewhere. —*Madame Bovary* (1857), Gustave Flaubert

CHEAT SHEET V: SOME FOODS OF THE BRITISH ISLES

Angels on horseback: A savory dish of broiled or grilled bacon-wrapped oysters, served as an appetizer or after the entrée.

Black bun: Yeast-leavened egg bread dough darkened with sweet spices, candied fruit, and chopped nuts, wrapped in a thin layer of plain dough and then baked, cut into wedges, and served with afternoon tea.

Black pudding: Northern English sausage made with pig's blood, oatmeal, pork fat, onions, and herbs. The sausage is first boiled whole and then sliced and pan-fried.

Bubble and squeak: Leftover chopped potatoes and cabbage or Brussels sprouts, sautéed in beef suet or bacon drippings.

Champ: Irish mashed potatoes with scallions, milk, and a pool of melted butter.

Clotted cream: A specialty of Cornwall and Devon; unpasteurized cream that has been scalded and then chilled, giving it a thick texture and sweet flavor.

Cock-a-leekie: Scottish chicken soup with leeks, sometimes prepared with oatmeal or prunes.

Colcannon: *Champ* with the addition of cabbage.

Cornish pasty: A pastry turnover filled with meat and potatoes, originated as an economical, filling, convenient lunch for coal miners in Cornwall.

Crumpet: Soda-leavened tea bread cooked on a griddle, resulting in a hole-riddled texture that soaks up butter or jam.

Dublin coddle: A simple stew of sausage, bacon, and onions.

Finnan haddie: Smoked haddock, usually served at breakfast.

Fool: Pureed cooked fruit blended with whipped cream or custard, then chilled.

Haggis: Scottish specialty of lamb's liver and other variety meats, minced and mixed with suet, oatmeal, onion, and spices, then stuffed into a sheep's stomach and simmered for several hours.

Jugged: Refers to game, usually hare, or other meat marinated with vinegar or red wine in an earthenware crock (the jug) and then slowly braised.

Kedgeree: Named after and adapted from the Indian lentil-and-rice *khichari*, this breakfast or brunch dish combines flaked smoked haddock, rice, curry spices, and hard-boiled egg.

Kipper: A brined and smoked herring, served for breakfast.

Mulligatawny soup: A spicy blend of chicken or meat broth, onions, mild spices, and yogurt, coconut milk, or cream, adapted from colonial Indian influences, with a name derived from the Tamil *milakutanni,* "pepper water."

Scone: A soda-leavened teacake shaped into discs or wedges

Scotch egg: Hard-boiled egg enclosed in fresh sausage meat and bread crumbs, then deep-fried; usually served cold as a pub lunchtime offering.

Toad-in-the-hole: Sausages baked in Yorkshire pudding batter.

Trifle: Dessert composed of layers of sherry-soaked sponge cake, jam, fruit, custard, and whipped cream.

Yorkshire pudding: A batter of flour, eggs, and milk, cooked in beef drippings until puffy and golden brown, and served as an accompaniment to roast beef.

Welsh rabbit (or "rarebit"): Shredded Cheddar cheese mixed with mustard, Worcestershire sauce, and other seasonings, then melted over toast.

GARGANTUA'S[1] PANTRY

In a cellar of Gargantuan abode he hid away a fine heap of red wheat, beside twenty jars of mustard and several delicacies, such as plums and Tourainian rolls[2], articles of a dessert, Olivet cheese[3], goat cheese, and others, well known between Langeais and Loches[4], pots of butter, hare pasties, preserved ducks, pigs' trotters in bran, boatloads and pots full of crushed peas, pretty little pots of Orleans quince preserve, hogsheads of lampreys[5], measures of green sauce, river game, such as francolins[6], teal, sheldrake, heron, and flamingo, all preserved in sea-salt, dried raisins, tongues smoked in the manner invented by Happe-Mousche, his celebrated ancestor, and sweetstuff for Garga-melle on feast days; and a thousand other things.

—"The Sermon of the Merry Vicar of Meudon," Honoré de Balzac (1799–1850)

1. The giant Gargantua, a character immortalized in the stories of François Rabelais (approximately 1483–1553) and source of the adjective "gargantuan," which certainly applied to his appetite for food and drink.
2. Most likely whole wheat breads made with honey and spice, in the style of the Touraine region of France's Loire Valley.
3. A soft cheese named for the town of Olivet in the Orléans region of central France, made in late spring from extra-rich cow's milk
4. Two towns of the Loire Valley, a region famed for its goat's milk cheeses.
5. Barrels filled with a particular type of eel.
6. Members of the pheasant family.

ACTIVE INGREDIENTS: SOME CHEMICAL COMPOUNDS

CH_3COOH: Acetic acid, the acid in vinegar.

$C_3H_6O_3$: Lactic acid, the acid found in soured milk and also pickles formed by acid fermentation such as sauerkraut and Korean kimchee.

$C_8H_{10}N_4O_2$: Caffeine, the alkaloid stimulant found in coffee, tea, chocolate, and cola.

$C_6H_{12}O_6$: Glucose and fructose, the form of sugar found in fruits, honey, and corn syrup.

$C_{12}H_{22}O_{11}$: Sucrose, the most familiar form of sugar.

C_2H_5OH: Ethyl alcohol, the potable alcohol of wine, beer, and spirits.

$C_6H_8O_7$: Citric acid, the mild acid found in lemons and other citrus fruits.

CO_2: Carbon dioxide, the gas in sparkling wine, beer, soda water, and soft drinks.

H_2O: Water.

KNO_2: Potassium nitrite, a preservative used for meats and sausages used in small quantities to maintain a fresh red color.

NaCl: Sodium chloride, also known as salt.

$NaHCO_3$: Sodium bicarbonate, or baking soda, used to leaven quick breads.

EVERY SYMPTOM OF AUTUMN'S CULINARY ABUNDANCE

As Ichabod jogged slowly on his way his eye, ever open to every symptom of culinary abundance, ranged with delight over the treasures of jolly Autumn. On all sides he beheld vast store of apples—some hanging in oppressive opulence on the trees, some gathered into baskets and barrels for the market, others heaped up in rich piles for the cider-press. Farther on he beheld great fields of Indian corn, with its golden ears peeping from their leafy coverts and holding out the promise of cakes and hasty pudding; and the yellow pumpkins lying beneath them, turning up their fair round bellies to the sun, and giving ample prospects of the most luxurious of pies; and anon he passed the fragrant buckwheat-fields, breathing the odor of the beehive, and as he beheld them soft anticipations stole over his mind of dainty slapjacks, well buttered and garnished with honey or treacle by the delicate little dimpled hand of Katrina Van Tassel.

—"The Legend of Sleepy Hollow," *The Sketch Book of Geoffrey Crayon, Gent.* (1819–1820), Washington Irving

FUN WITH FOOD & DRINK, PART III:
HOW TO FORCE AN EGG INTO A MILK BOTTLE

It may seem like a physical impossibility: an entire hard-boiled egg sitting inside a classic glass milk bottle with a neck narrower than the egg's diameter. Such physical barriers, however, may be skirted thanks to the relative plasticity of the egg—minus its shell, of course—and by creating differences in air pressure.

1. **Find the right bottle.** Look in the supermarket for milk in a classic bottle with thick glass walls and a neck about one and a half inches in diameter. These are still used for some organic and other small-dairy milks, and may be found in natural foods stores. Buy it, use the milk, and clean and dry the bottle.

2. **Prepare the egg.** Place a whole egg in a small saucepan of cold water. Bring the water to a boil, reduce the heat to a simmer, and cook until the egg is hard-boiled, about seven minutes. Drain and rinse the egg under cold running water, then refrigerate in its shell.

3. **Peel and chill the egg.** Fill a bowl with ice and water. Remove the egg from the refrigerator, tap its shell all around on the kitchen counter to break it, and then peel off the shell under cold running water. Put the whole peeled egg into the ice water, leaving it only as long as it takes to prepare the bottle.

4. **Warm the bottle.** Protecting your hands with kitchen gloves, turn on a stream of the hottest water possible. Rinse the empty milk bottle inside and out under the water for about one minute, then empty the bottle and place it on the kitchen counter.

5. **Position the egg.** Immediately remove the egg from the ice water and place it narrow end down on the opening of the bottle. The hot air inside the bottle, being at a lower pressure than the cooler air temperature around the egg and its surroundings, will cause the exterior air to push the egg into the bottle. (If this does not work, due to atmospheric or weather conditions or the heat of the water in your kitchen sink, instead carefully light two wooden kitchen matches and drop them into the dry, clean bottle; then, immediately place the chilled and dried egg on top of the bottle.)

SOME EATING WORLD RECORDS

This list has been compiled from various authoritative sources. For updates of records set in officially sanctioned events, visit www.ifoce.com, Web site of the International Federation of Competitive Eating, the New York City–based organization that "supervises and regulates eating contests in their various forms throughout the world." (Note that these records have been set by dedicated competitors who train seriously and carefully for their events. Amateurs attempting to break such records may become seriously ill.)

Item	Amount	Time (mins:secs)	Record Holder
Single Ingredients			
Brussels sprouts	43	1:00	Dave Mynard
Butter (¼-lb sticks)	7	5:00	Donald Lerman
Cabbage	6 lb 9 oz	9:00	Charles Hardy
Chocolate candy bars	2 lb	6:00	Eric Booker
Corn on the cob (ears)	33½	12:00	Cookie Jarvis
Cow brains	57 (17.7 lb)	15:00	Takeru Kobayashi
Crawfish	331	12:00	Chris Hendrix
Eggs, hard-boiled	65	6:40	Sonya Thomas
Jalapeño chilies	8	1:00	Anita Crafford
	152	15:00	Jed Donahue
Mayonnaise	1 gal	8:00	Oleg Zhornitskiy
Oysters, raw	97	3:00	John Wright
	36 dozen (432)	10:00	Sonya Thomas
Pickles, sour	2½ pounds	5:00	Kevin Lipsitz
Prepared Foods			
Beans, baked	6 lb	1:48	Donald Lerman
Beef tongue, pickled	3 lb 3 oz	12:00	Dominic Cardo
Chicken wings	137	30:00	Bill Simmons
Chicken wings, buffalo	94	12:00	Cookie Jarvis
Conch fritters	45	6:00	Joe Menchetti
Corn dogs	12	10:00	Richard LeFevre
Corned beef hash	4 lb	10:00	Eric Booker
Doughnuts, glazed	49	8:00	Eric Booker
Dumplings, Chinese	91	8:00	Cookie Jarvis

Item	Amount	Time (mins:secs)	Record Holder
Jell-O	121 oz	1:30	Steve Lakind
Gelatine, sweet	7 lb	3:00	Steve Lakind
Hamburgers (¼-lb)	11¼	10:00	Donald Lerman
Hamburgers (¾-lb)	7	10:00	Sonya Thomas
Hot dogs and buns	53½	12:00	Takeru Kobayashi
Ice cream, vanilla	1 gal 9 oz	12:00	Cookie Jarvis
Jambalaya, crawfish	9 lb	10:00	Sonya Thomas
Matzo balls	21	5:25	Eric Booker
Mince pie	2½ lb	:30	Peter Dowdeswell
Pulled-pork sandwiches	23	10:00	Sonya Thomas
Rice balls	20 lb	30:00	Takeru Kobayashi
SPAM, canned	6 lb	12:00	Richard LeFevre

SOME NATIONAL FOOD OBSERVANCES: JULY

Entire month:

National Baked Bean Month
National Culinary Arts Month
National Hot Dog Month
National Ice Cream Month
National July Belongs to Blueberries Month

Third Sunday of the month:

National Ice Cream Day

6th:	National Fried Chicken Day
7th:	National Strawberry Sundae Day
9th:	National Sugar Cookie Day
12th:	National Pecan Pie Day
15th:	National Tapioca Pudding Day
17th:	National Peach Ice Cream Day
18th:	National Caviar Day
20th:	National Lollipop Day
21st:	National Hot Dog Day
23rd:	National Vanilla Ice Cream Day
28th:	National Drive-Thru Day
	National Milk Chocolate Day
30th:	National Cheesecake Day

GREAT AMERICAN DINER SLANG

From the early days of the great American diner in the 1920s until diner culture began to dwindle in the 1970s, its cooks and wait staff evolved a delightful, sometimes poetic shorthand slang to describe staple menu items and other aspects of this particular restaurant experience. Some of the terminology derived from African American waiter lingo of the 19th century. (For even more slang and diner history, visit www.dinermuseum.org.)

For Breakfast
Adam and Eve on a raft: Two poached eggs on a slice of toast.
Bailed hay: Shredded wheat.
Blowout patches: Pancakes.
Burn the British: Toasted English muffin.
Cackle fruit: Eggs.
Clean the kitchen: Hash.
Dead eye: Poached egg.
Dough well done with cow to cover: Buttered toast.
Life preserver: Doughnut.
Looseners: Stewed prunes.
Noah's boy: Ham.
Over easy: Eggs fried and flipped over to cook the yolks a bit more.
Over hard: Eggs fried and flipped over to cook the yolks through.
Shingle with a shimmy and a shake: Buttered toast with jelly.
Stack of Vermont: Pancakes with maple syrup.
Sunny side up: Eggs fried unflipped with the yolks runny.
Sweepings: Hash.
Whiskey down: Rye toast.
Wreck 'em: Scrambled eggs.

For Lunch
BLT: Bacon, lettuce, and tomato sandwich.
Bow-wow: Hot dog.
Bowl of red: Chili con carne.
Burn one: Grill a burger.
Burn one, take it through the garden, and pin a rose on it: Burger with lettuce, tomato, and onion.
Chewed with fine breath: Burger with onions.
Coney Island: Hot dog.
GAC: Grilled American cheese sandwich.
Ground hog: Hot dog.
Hockey puck: Well-done hamburger.
Jack Benny: Grilled cheese sandwich with bacon.
One from the Alps: Swiss cheese sandwich.
Tube steak: Hot dog.
Radio: Tuna ("tuner") sandwich.

For Dinner
Bloodhounds in the hay: Frankfurters and sauerkraut.
Blue plate special: Daily special, usually meat with potato and vegetable.

Bossy in a bowl: Beef stew.
First lady: Spareribs.
Foreign entanglements: Spaghetti.
Hounds on an island: Frankfurters and beans.
Irish turkey: Corned beef and cabbage.
Put out the lights and cry: Liver and onions.
SOS: Chipped or ground beef in gravy on toast.
Well-dressed diner: Codfish.
Zeppelins in a fog: Sausages and mashed potatoes.

On the Side and Extras
All hot: Baked potato.
Breath: Onion.
Bullets: Baked beans.
Cow feed: Salad.
Dog biscuits: Crackers.
Frenchman's delight: Pea soup.
Frog sticks: French fries.
Murphy: Baked potato.
Rabbit food: Lettuce.
Splash of red noise: Tomato soup.
Wax: American cheese.
Whistleberries: Baked beans.
Wreath: Cabbage or coleslaw.

For Dessert
China: Rice pudding.
Cold mud: Chocolate ice cream.
Eve with a lid on: Apple pie.
Eve with a moldy lid: Apple pie with cheese.
Fish eyes: Tapioca pudding.
Fly cake: Raisin cake.
Ice the rice: Rice pudding à la mode.

Magoo: Custard pie.
Nervous pudding: Gelatin.
Sleigh ride special: Vanilla pudding.

Beverages
Adam's ale: Water.
Atlanta special: Coca-Cola.
Balloon juice: Seltzer or carbonated water.
Belch water: Seltzer or carbonated water.
Billiard: Buttermilk.
Blonde with sand: Coffee with cream and sugar.
Boiled leaves: Tea.
City juice: Water.
Cow juice: Milk.
Creep: Draft beer.
Cup of mud: Coffee.
Dog soup: Water.
Drag one through Georgia: Coca-Cola with chocolate syrup.
Fifty-five: Root beer.
Flowing Mississippi: Black coffee.
Hot top: Hot chocolate.
Java: Coffee.
Joe: Coffee.
M.D.: Dr. Pepper.
Moo juice: Milk.
Oh gee: Orange juice.
Shake one in the hay: Strawberry milkshake.
Shoot from the South: Fountain Coca-Cola.
Spot with a twist: Tea with lemon.
Squeeze one: Orange juice.
Sun kiss: Orange juice.
Sweet Alice: Milk.
Windmill cocktail: Water.

Special Ingredients
Axle grease: Butter.
Bronx vanilla: Garlic.
Canned cow: Evaporated milk.
Cow paste: Butter.
Hail: Ice.
Halitosis: Garlic.
Hemorrhage: Ketchup.
Machine oil: Syrup.
Mud: Chocolate syrup.
Sand: Sugar.
Sea dust: Salt.
Skid grease: Butter.
Smear: Margarine.
Warts: Olives.
Yellow paint: Mustard.
Yum yum: Sugar.

Special Requests
Eighty-six: Remove from the menu; out of stock.
High and dry: Hold the butter, mayonnaise, and lettuce from a sandwich.
Hold the hail: Without ice.
In the alley: Serve on the side.

Keep off the grass: Hold the lettuce.
Let it walk: Pack an item to go.
Make it cry: Add onion.
No cow: Hold the milk.
On the hoof: Cook it rare.
Paint it red: Put ketchup on it.
Pittsburgh: Well-charred on the outside, rare inside.
Throw it in the mud: Add chocolate syrup.

The Staff
Angel: Sandwich maker.
Bubble dancer: Dishwasher.
Ladybug: Soda fountain man.
Soup jockey: Waitress.

The Setting and Equipment
Chopper: Knife.
Gallery: Booth.
Lighthouse: Ketchup bottle.
Lumber: Toothpick.
Mike and Ike: Salt and pepper shakers.
Radar range: Microwave.
The twins: Salt and pepper shakers.

THE CONSOLATION OF MUFFINS

Algernon: I don't think there is much likelihood, Jack, of you and Miss Fairfax being united.

Jack: Well, that is no business of yours.

Algernon: If it was my business, I wouldn't talk about it. [Begins to eat muffins.] It is very vulgar to talk about one's business. Only people like stock-brokers do that, and then merely at dinner parties.

Jack: How can you sit there, calmly eating muffins when we are in this horrible trouble, I can't make out. You seem to me to be perfectly heartless.

Algernon: Well, I can't eat muffins in an agitated manner. The butter would probably get on my cuffs. One should always eat muffins quite calmly. It is the only way to eat them.

Jack: I say it's perfectly heartless your eating muffins at all, under the circumstances.

Algernon: When I am in trouble, eating is the only thing that consoles me. Indeed, when I am in really great trouble, as any one who knows me intimately will tell you, I refuse everything except food and drink. At the present moment I am eating muffins because I am unhappy. Besides, I am particularly fond of muffins. [Rising.]

Jack: [Rising.] Well, that is no reason why you should eat them all in that greedy way. [Takes muffins from ALGERNON.]

Algernon: [Offering tea-cake.] I wish you would have tea-cake instead. I don't like tea-cake.

Jack: Good heavens! I suppose a man may eat his own muffins in his own garden.

Algernon: But you have just said it was perfectly heartless to eat muffins.

Jack: I said it was perfectly heartless of you, under the circumstances. That is a very different thing.

Algernon: That may be. But the muffins are the same. [He seizes the muffin-dish from JACK.]

—*The Importance of Being Earnest*, Act II, Part 2 (1895), Oscar Wilde

THE DINNER OF THE THREE EMPERORS

Served at the Café Anglais, Paris, on June 7, 1867, to Russian Tsar Alexander II; his son, the future Tsar Alexander III; and Prussian Kaiser Wilhelm I. The total check for the trio came to 1,200 francs, equivalent to more than $13,000 today.

Hors-d'Oeuvre
Potage Imperatrice[1]
Soufflé à la Reine[2]

◆

Releves
Filets de Sole à la Vénitienne[3]
Escalope de Turbot au Gratin
Selle de Mouton Puree Breton [4]

◆

Entrees
Poulet à la Portugaise[5]
Pâté Chaud de Cailles[6]
Homard à la Parisienne[7]
Sorbets au Champagne

◆

Roties
Canetons à la Rouennaise[8]
Ortolans sur Canapés[9]

◆

Entremets
Aubergine à l'Espagnole[10]
Asperges en Branches[11]
Cassolettes Princesse[12]
Bombe Glacée[13]

◆

Vins
Madère Retour de l'Inde, 1810[14]
Xérès Retour de l'Inde, 1821
Chateau d'Yquem, 1847
Chambertin, 1846
Chateau Margaux, 1847

Chateau-Latour 1847
Chateau Lafite, 1848
Champagne Roederer

1. A chicken consommé garnished with cocks' combs and kidneys, asparagus tips, and fresh chervil leaves.
2. A soufflé of minced chicken or turkey and ham.
3. Sole fillets poached and served with a rich sauce of broth, eggs, butter, tarragon vinegar, and fresh tarragon.
4. Saddle of lamb served with pureed white beans.
5. Chicken served with a rich, thick tomato sauce.
6. Hot pâté of quail.
7. Poached and shelled lobster, served cold, glazed with fish aspic, and garnished with vegetables and truffles.
8. Duckling stuffed, roasted, and served with a spicy sauce of reduced red wine, stock, and chicken livers.
9. Small wild birds cooked and eaten whole.
10. Eggplant cooked with tomatoes, peppers, onions, and garlic.
11. Whole cooked asparagus spears.
12. A rich egg custard served in small porcelain dishes with short handles.
13. A frozen molded ice cream.
14. *Retour de l'Inde*, "returned from India," refers to the late 18th century discovery that fortified wines, particularly Madeira, improved in flavor after an ocean voyage to India and back.

SOME BEER-DERIVED TURNS OF PHRASE

Mind your p's and q's: Meaning "to behave and mind one's own business," this comes from a traditional English pub keeper's admonition to unruly customers to calm down by paying attention only to the pints and quarts of beer they were drinking.

Rule of thumb: Meaning "a general guideline," the phrase comes from the old brewer's practice of gauging the brewing temperature of beer for the safe addition of yeast by dipping a thumb into the liquid.

Wet your whistle: Meaning "to satisfy one's thirst," this comes from the fact that, centuries ago, pub regulars had special beer tankards with whistles built into the rims, which they would blow to summon a refill.

CHEAT SHEET VI: SOME ITALIAN FOODS

Aglio e olio: Pasta sauced with chopped garlic sautéed in olive oil.

Agrodolce: Sweet-and-sour cooking sauce for meat or vegetables, featuring red wine, vinegar, olive oil, onion, sugar or honey, lemon zest, and such other ingredients as raisins, pine nuts, and sometimes chocolate.

Alfredo: Pasta, usually fresh fettuccine, tossed with grated Parmesan, butter, and sometimes cream.

Amaretti: Crisp little cookies made with ground kernels from apricot pits or bitter almonds, egg whites, and sugar.

Amatriciana: Pasta sauce of tomatoes, olive oil, onion, and bacon or salt pork, in the style of the town of Amatrice, near Rome.

Arrabbiata: Tomato sauce, usually for pasta, made "rabid" with hot chili flakes.

Bagna cauda: A "hot bath" of olive oil, butter, garlic, anchovies, and white truffle, served as a dip.

Bollito misto: A "mixed boil" of meats, chicken, or tongue, simmered with vegetables and seasonings. The cooking broth is served first, followed by the sliced meats and a salsa verde of capers, garlic, shallots, anchovies, olive oil, and lemon juice.

Bolognese: Called *ragù* in its native Bologna, this thick mixed-meat-and-tomato sauce is a favorite to serve with pasta.

Cacciatore: Hunter-style treatment for poultry, meat, or seafood, involving cooking with tomatoes and wine, plus usually peppers and garlic.

Cannoli: Fried or baked pastry tube filled with sweet ricotta cheese mixture.

Caponata: Sweet-sour stew of eggplants, tomatoes, and other vegetables.

Carbonara: "Charcoal-maker's" style of pasta, tossed with bacon or salt pork, olive oil, beaten egg, Parmesan cheese, and freshly ground black pepper.

Carpaccio: Raw beef sliced translucently thin, garnished with capers, anchovies, chives, mustard, and other piquant accompaniments.

Fiorentina: Florence-style, referring usually to broiled or roasted steak or other meats seasoned with olive oil, rosemary, garlic, and lemon.

Fritto misto: A "mixed fry" of batter-dipped or lightly floured pieces of seafood and vegetables.

Frittata: A flat, thick omelet with eggs and filling mixed together.

Gnocchi: Little boiled or baked dumplings served as a pasta course, usually made from wheat flour, mashed potato, and egg.

Granita: A "grainy" iced dessert made by freezing and repeatedly scraping with a fork a syrup-based mixture, usually flavored with fruit juice, coffee, or chocolate, to form icy crystals that are then scooped up and served.

Gremolata: Grated lemon or orange zest mixed with chopped parsley and garlic as an aromatic garnish for *osso buco* or other dishes.

Marinara: A "sailor-style" sauce of tomatoes, garlic, olive oil, and basil, usually for pasta.

Osso buco: Meaning "hollow bone," a Milanese braise of bone-in veal shanks cooked with wine, stocks, tomatoes, onions, garlic, and herbs until fall-apart tender, topped with *gremolata*, and served with *polenta* or *risotto*.

Pesto: A traditional sauce from Genoa, made by pounding together fresh basil, garlic, pine nuts, Parmesan cheese, and olive oil.

Polenta: A thick cornmeal porridge, usually served as an accompaniment to savory main courses; or cooled until firm, cut into shapes, sautéed or baked, and served with butter and cheese or tomato sauce.

Risotto: A northern specialty consisting of Arborio rice, or other varieties with short, plump, starchy grains, cooked in broth and wine until it is tender-chewy and its surface starch forms a rich, creamy sauce.

Romana: "Roman style" of cooking, usually featuring butter and Parmesan, or ricotta cheese, or tomatoes, ham, onions, peppers, and garlic.

EATING AND DRINKING ACROSS THE MAP, PART V: BAKERY AND PASTRY DEPARTMENT

Biscuit Basin, Wyoming
Biscuit Bayou, Louisiana
Biscuit Brook, New York,
Biscuit Butte, Montana (also Oregon)
Biscuit Creek, Idaho (also Kansas, Michigan, and Oregon)
Biscuit Hill, Arizona
Bread Loaf, Vermont
Bread Springs, New Mexico
Bread Tray Hill, Alabama
Brownie Branch, Mississippi
Brownie Butte, Montana
Brownie Creek, Alaska (also California, Montana, Nevada, Oregon, and Washington)

Cake Hill, Wyoming
Cake Mountain, Arizona
Cake Rock, Washington
Cookietown, Oklahoma
Cracker, Montana
Donut Island, Minnesota
Donut Lake, Michigan (also Minnesota)
Donut Rock, California
Muffin Butte, Utah
Muffin Islands, Alaska
Pie, West Virginia
Roll, Arizona (also Indiana and Oklahoma)
Scone, New South Wales, Australia
Tortilla Flat, Arizona

FOOD AND DRINK IN SHAKESPEARE'S PLAYS

No surprise that the greatest playwright of all time and master chronicler of life in the Elizabethan age should include food and drink and eating and drinking frequently in his works, as dramatic devices, as puns, and as metaphors. A random selection of examples (dates shown are for first performances):

The Comedy of Errors (1592)
Small cheer and great welcome makes a merry feast.
(Act III, Scene 1)

Thou say'st his meat was sauced with thy upbraidings:
Unquiet meals make ill digestions.
(Act V, Scene 1)

◆

The Taming of the Shrew (1593)
What say you to a piece of beef and mustard?
(Act IV, Scene 3)

◆

Love's Labours Lost (1594)
An I had but one penny in the world, thou shouldst have it for gingerbread.
(Act V, Scene 1)

◆

Romeo and Juliet (1594)
Thy head is as full of quarrels as an egg is full of meat, and yet thy head hath been beaten as addle as an egg for quarrelling.
(Act III, Scene 1)

They call for dates and quinces in the pastry.
(Act IV, Scene 4)

A Midsummer Night's Dream (1595)

And most dear actors, eat no onions nor garlic
for we are to utter sweet breath.
(Act IV, Scene 2)

◆

Henry IV, Part 1 (1597)

If sack and sugar be a fault, God help the wicked!
(Act III, Scene 3)

◆

Henry IV, Part 2 (1598)

He hath eaten me out of house and home.
(Act II, Scene 1)

That's a marvellous searching wine, and it perfumes
the blood 'ere one can say, 'What's this?'
(Act II, Scene 4)

◆

Henry V (1599)

The strawberry grows underneath the nettle
And wholesome berries thrive and ripen best
Neighbour'd by fruit of baser quality.
(Act 1, Scene 1)

Then give them great meals of beef and iron and steel,
they will eat like wolves and fight like devils.
(Act III, Scene 7)

◆

The Merry Wives of Windsor (1600)

Come, we have a hot venison pasty to dinner: come, gentlemen,
I hope we shall drink down all unkindness.
(Act I, Scene 1)

I will make an end of my dinner;
there's pippins and cheese to come.
(Act I, Scene 2)

Why, then the world's mine oyster, which I with sword will open.
(Act II, Scene 2)

'Tis time I were choked with a piece of toasted cheese.
(Act V, Scene 5)

◆

Twelfth Night (1602)
I am a great eater of beef, and I believe that does harm to my wit.
(Act I, Scene 3)

◆

Troilus and Cressida (1602)
I'll heat his blood with Greekish wine to-night,
Which with my scimitar I'll cool to-morrow.
Patroclus, let us feast him to the height.
(Act V, Scene 1)

◆

All's Well That Ends Well (1603)
Mine eyes smell onions; I shall weep anon.
(Act V, Scene 3)

◆

Othello (1604)
Come, come, good wine is a good familiar creature
if it be well used; exclaim no more against it.
(Act II, Scene 3)

I have very poor and unhappy brains for drinking: I could well wish
courtesy would invent some other custom of entertainment.
(Act II, Scene 3)

◆

Antony and Cleopatra (**1606**)
I love long life better than figs.
(Act I, Scene 2)

◆

The Winter's Tale (**1610**)
For a quart of ale is a dish for a king.
(Act IV, Scene 2)

Let me see; what am I to buy for
our sheep-shearing feast? Three pound of sugar, five pound
of currants, rice,—what will this sister of mine do with rice? But my
father hath made her mistress of the feast, and she lays it on. . . .
I must have saffron to colour the warden pies; mace; dates, none;
that's out of my note; nutmegs seven; a race or two of ginger,
but that I may beg; four pound of prunes, and as
many of raisins o' the sun.
(Act IV, Scene 2)

◆

The Tempest (**1611**)
I'll shew thee the best springs; I'll pluck thee berries.
(Act II, Scene 2)

Ceres, most bounteous lady, thy rich leas
Of wheat, rye, barley, vetches, oats and pease;
Thy turfy mountains, where live nibbling sheep . . .
(Act IV, Scene 1)

SOME MILESTONES IN FOOD AND DRINK HISTORY:
16TH CENTURY AD

1511: Khair Beg, corrupt governor of Mecca, attempts unsuccessfully to ban coffee.

1516: Bavaria's Duke Wilhelm IV issues the Rheinheitsgebot (see page 113), a beer purity law that constitutes the first public act of consumer protection.

1519: A member of Hernando Cortés's Spanish expedition to Mexico witnesses the Aztec King Montezuma drinking a thick, spicy, hot beverage called *xocoatl,* made from cacao beans: hot chocolate.

1523: Turkeys from the New World are brought to Spain, and their use spreads to England and other Old World countries.

1525: Portuguese traders introduce chili peppers to India.

1527: Spanish conquistadors bring home papayas, avocados, and tomatoes.

1532: Florentine aristocrat Caterina de' Medici, age 14, marries future King Henri II of France, bringing with her to the French court expert Italian cooks who will revolutionize French cuisine.

1538: Iberian explorers introduce peanuts to China.

1539: Members of Camille Pizarro's expedition bring potatoes from Peru to Spain.

1559: Italians begin to make gelato.

1582: The famed Tour d'Argent restaurant opens in Paris.

1588: In the wreckage from the Spanish Armada, potatoes reputedly come ashore in Ireland.

1592: The brewery that will become Heineken is founded in Holland.

1599: Sir Edward Kennel, commander of Britain's Royal Navy, develops punch as a celebratory drink.

A FONDNESS FOR MELONS

A very fine man, Ivan Ivanovitch! He is very fond of melons: they are his favourite food. As soon as he has dined, and come out on his balcony, in his shirt sleeves, he orders Gapka to bring two melons, and immediately cuts them himself, collects the seeds in a paper, and begins to eat. Then he orders Gapka to fetch the ink-bottle, and, with his own hand, writes this inscription on the paper of seeds: "These melons were eaten on such and such a date." If there was a guest present, then it reads, "Such and such a person assisted."   —"How the Two Ivans Quarrelled" (1834), Nikolai Gogol

FUN WITH FOOD & DRINK, PART IV:
HOW TO GROW A PINEAPPLE

As their spiky crowns of leaves suggest, pineapples are the fruit of a plant related to bromeliads, the family of tropical plants that send out outlandish-looking flower stalks. You can grow an attractive houseplant from the top of a store-bought pineapple:

1. **Pick a fruit.** Start with a fresh, whole pineapple. At the store, look for one that is slightly unripe, with deep-green leaves and skin that is still slightly green. Look closely at the base of the leaves, and avoid any with signs of gray scales, a common plant malady.
2. **Slice off the crown.** With a sharp knife, slice off the entire crown of leaves at the point where it joins the fruit, leaving no fruit attached.
3. **Trim to the core.** One at a time, starting at the base of the crown, strip off the outer leaves, until you reach a central core of about six smaller leaves attached to the bulblike stem.
4. **Dry it.** Set this aside in a cool, dark, dry place for five to seven days, until the stem surface looks firm and dry.
5. **Sprout roots.** Suspend the stem in a jar, immersing its end in about half an inch of water, with the leaves clear of the water. Place at room temperature away from direct sunlight until roots have sprouted, two to four weeks.
6. **Plant it.** Plant the pineapple in a pot with good drainage, filled with two parts commercial potting compound designed for bromeliads or cacti, mixed with one part perlite. Keep the soil consistently just moist but not wet, watering about once a week but more often if necessary in warmer months. When you see new leaves growing from the center, you'll know your pineapple has taken root.
7. **Give it light.** Allow the pineapple six hours of bright light daily. Repot as growth necessitates.
8. **Force flowers and fruit.** To force a mature plant to flower and bear fruit, in winter enclose it for two weeks in a paper bag with two ripe bruised apples. They'll release ethylene gas, which triggers the flowering process. Return the plant to its usual spot and routine, and two to three months later a flower spike should emerge from the center, and a pineapple will develop at the end.

ROBERT BURNS'S "ADDRESS TO A HAGGIS"

In 1786, the great Scottish poet Robert Burns (1759–1796) composed one of his most famous odes in celebration of his nation's glorious (or, to some tastes, odious) boiled pudding of sheep's innards, fat, oatmeal, and spices. Nowadays, Scots traditionally recite the poem on Burns Night, January 25, the poet's birthday, which is celebrated with a dinner featuring haggis as the main course. Bashed neeps (mashed turnips) and great lashings of single-malt Scotch whiskey are the traditional accompaniments, the latter a proven way to anesthetize diners less sympathetic to the haggis.

> Fair fa'[1] your honest, sonsie[2] face,
> Great chieftain o' the puddin'-race!
> Aboon[3] them a' ye tak your place,
> Painch,[4] tripe, or thairm:[5]
> Weel[6] are ye wordy[7] of a grace
> As lang's my arm.
>
> The groaning trencher there ye fill,
> Your hurdies[8] like a distant hill,
> Your pin[9] wad help to mend a mill
> In time o' need,
> While thro' your pores the dews distil
> Like amber bead.
>
> His knife see Rustic-labour dight,[10]
> An' cut you up wi' ready slight,[11]
> Trenching[12] your gushing entrails bright
> Like onie[13] ditch;
> And then, O what a glorious sight,
> Warm-reekin, rich!
>
> Then, horn[14] for horn they stretch an' strive,
> Deil tak[15] the hindmost, on they drive,
> Till a' their weel-swall'd kytes[16] belyve[17]
> Are bent like drums;
> Then auld Guidman[18], maist[19] like to rive,[20]
> 'Bethankit'[21] hums.

Is there that owre his French ragout,
Or olio that wad staw[22] a sow,
Or fricassee wad mak her spew
Wi' perfect sconner,[23]
Looks down wi' sneering, scornful' view
On sic[24] a dinner?

Poor devil! see him owre his trash,
As feckless[25] as a wither'd rash,
His spindle shank a guid whip-lash,
His nieve[26] a nit;[27]
Thro' bluidy flood or field to dash,
O how unfit!

But mark the Rustic, haggis-fed,
The trembling earth resounds his tread,
Clap in his walie[28] nieve[29] a blade,
He'll mak it whissle;
An' legs, an' arms, an' heads will sned,[30]
Like taps o' thrissle.[31]

Ye Pow'rs wha mak mankind your care,
And dish them out their bill o' fare,
Auld Scotland wants nae shinking[32] ware
That jaups in luggies;[33]
But, if you wish her gratefu' pray'r,
Gie her a Haggis!

1. Fall. 2. Cheery. 3. Above. 4. Paunch. 5. Guts. 6. Well. 7. Worthy. 8. Buttocks. 9. Skewer. 10. Wipe. 11. Skill. 12. Digging. 13. Any. 14. Spoon. 15. Devil take. 16. Well-swollen bellies. 17. By and by. 18. Goodman. 19. Almost. 20. Burst. 21. God be thanked. 22. Sicken. 23. Disgust. 24. Such. 25. Weakly. 26. Fist. 27. Nut. 28. Ample. 29. Fist. 30. Chop off. 31. Thistle tops. 32. Watery. 33. Splashes in porringers.

SOME NATIONAL FOOD OBSERVANCES: AUGUST

Entire month:

National Catfish Month
National Water Quality Month

1st: National Raspberry Cream Pie Day
2nd: National Ice Cream Sandwich Day
National Ice Cream Soda Day
3rd: National Bratwurst Day
National Watermelon Day
4th: National Chocolate Chip Day
5th: National Waffle Day
6th: National Root Beer Float Day
7th: National Mustard Day
National Raspberries and Cream Day
11th: National Kool-Aid Day
13th: National Filet Mignon Day
14th: National Creamsicle Day
15th: National Lemon Meringue Pie Day
18th: National Ice Cream Pie Day
19th: National Soft Ice Cream Day
21st: National Spumoni Day
23rd: National Sponge Cake Day
24th: National Peach Pie Day
25th: National Banana Split Day
26th: National Cherry Popsicle Day
27th: National Pots de Crème Day
28th: National Cherry Turnover Day
30th: National Toasted Marshmallow Day
31st: National Trail Mix Day

CHEAT SHEET VII: PAN-ASIAN FOOD AND DRINK

Achar: Salad of raw or cooked vegetables marinated in white or cider vinegar, sugar, salt, ginger, and sometimes garlic.
Adobo: Sharp-tasting Philippine stew of chicken, pork, beef, or seafood, cooked with vinegar, soy sauce, garlic, and black pepper.

Gado-gado: Salad of mixed vegetables, boiled potatoes, fried or raw tofu, hard-boiled eggs, crisply fried onions and garlic, and hot peanut butter dressing.

Guoi coin: Vietnamese appetizer of soft edible rice paper wrapped around fresh vegetables, rice noodles, and cooked cold shrimp, pork, or chicken, served uncooked with sauces for dipping.

Kimchee: Korean white cabbage pickled with red chilies and garlic.

Krupuk: Puffy deep-fried chips made from a mixture of shrimp and manioc flour, served as an appetizer or a garnish in Indonesian cooking.

Mee krob: Thai specialty of transparent deep-fried rice noodles tossed with pork, shrimp, onions, garlic, and a sweet-and-sour sauce, then garnished with cilantro, bean sprouts, and chopped peanuts.

Pad thai: Literally "Thai noodles," a dish of flat rice stick noodles with deep-fried tofu cubes and shrimp, chicken, or meat, stir-fried with a sauce of tamarind, salty pungent fish sauce, sugar, lime juice, garlic, chilies, onions, and egg, then garnished with bean sprouts, scallions, peanuts, and fresh lime.

Pho: Vietnam's most popular national dish, a big bowl of fragrant broth, rice noodles, and thinly sliced beef, chicken, or other meat, garnished with bean sprouts, fresh chilies, basil, mint, and lime juice.

Rijsttafel: Dutch for "rice table," referring to a traditional Indonesian feast of many different spicy dishes accompanied by rice.

Saté: Indonesian-style kebabs, featuring small chunks or strips of meat, poultry, or seafood grilled on bamboo skewers and served with peanut sauce and a sweet-and-salty cucumber salad.

SUCH A CUP OF COFFEE

A cup of coffee—real coffee—home-browned, home-ground, homemade, that comes to you dark as a hazel-eye, but changes to a golden bronze as you temper it with cream that never cheated, but was real cream from its birth, thick, tenderly yellow, perfectly sweet, neither lumpy nor frothing on the Java: such a cup of coffee is a match for twenty blue devils, and will exorcise them all.　　　　—*Eyes and Ears* (1862), Henry Ward Beecher

GRUEL...AND UNUSUAL PUNISHMENT

The room in which the boys were fed, was a large stone hall, with a copper at one end: out of which the master, dressed in an apron for the purpose, and assisted by one or two women, ladled the gruel at mealtimes. Of this festive composition each boy had one porringer, and no more—except on occasions of great public rejoicing, when he had two ounces and a quarter of bread besides.

The bowls never wanted washing. The boys polished them with their spoons till they shone again; and when they had performed this operation (which never took very long, the spoons being nearly as large as the bowls), they would sit staring at the copper, with such eager eyes, as if they could have devoured the very bricks of which it was composed; employing themselves, meanwhile, in sucking their fingers most assiduously, with the view of catching up any stray splashes of gruel that might have been cast thereon. Boys have generally excellent appetites. Oliver Twist and his companions suffered the tortures of slow starvation for three months: at last they got so voracious and wild with hunger, that one boy, who was tall for his age, and hadn't been used to that sort of thing (for his father had kept a small cookshop), hinted darkly to his companions, that unless he had another basin of gruel per diem, he was afraid he might some night happen to eat the boy who slept next him, who happened to be a weakly youth of tender age. He had a wild, hungry eye; and they implicitly believed him. A council was held; lots were cast who should walk up to the master after supper that evening, and ask for more; and it fell to Oliver Twist.

The evening arrived; the boys took their places. The master, in his cook's uniform, stationed himself at the copper; his pauper assistants ranged themselves behind him; the gruel was served out; and a long grace was said over the short commons. The gruel disappeared; the boys whispered each other, and winked at Oliver; while his next neighbours nudged him. Child as he was, he was desperate with hunger, and reckless with misery. He rose from the table; and advancing to the master, basin and spoon in hand, said: somewhat alarmed at his own temerity:

'Please, sir, I want some more.'

The master was a fat, healthy man; but he turned very pale. He gazed in stupified astonishment on the small rebel for some seconds, and then clung for support to the copper. The assistants were paralysed with wonder; the boys with fear.

'What!' said the master at length, in a faint voice.

'Please, sir,' replied Oliver, 'I want some more.'

The master aimed a blow at Oliver's head with the ladle; pinioned him in his arm; and shrieked aloud for the beadle.

The board were sitting in solemn conclave, when Mr. Bumble rushed into the room in great excitement, and addressing the gentleman in the high chair, said,

'Mr. Limbkins, I beg your pardon, sir! Oliver Twist has asked for more!'

There was a general start. Horror was depicted on every countenance.

'For MORE!' said Mr. Limbkins. 'Compose yourself, Bumble, and answer me distinctly. Do I understand that he asked for more, after he had eaten the supper allotted by the dietary?'

'He did, sir,' replied Bumble.

'That boy will be hung,' said the gentleman in the white waistcoat. 'I know that boy will be hung.'   —*Oliver Twist* (1837–1839), Charles Dickens

MUSIC GOOD ENOUGH TO EAT

It's no surprise that musical groups have found inspiration, or at least metaphors, for their own names in popular foods and drinks. Herewith, two more-than-baker's dozens of examples, one savory and one sweet, verified via Apple's iTunes Music Store:

Savory
* Blue Tofu
* Bowling for Soup
* Bread
* The Chili Blues Band
* Drain the Lobster
* Gravy Train
* Hot Soup
* Hot Tuna
* Menudo
* Red Hot Chili Peppers
* Sandwich
* The String Cheese Incident
* Tastes Like Chicken
* The Truffles

Sweet
* The Banana Splits
* Blind Melon
* The Cranberries
* Hot Chocolate
* Humble Pie
* Lemonade Stand Band
* Liquid Pie
* The Marmalade
* Orange Cake Mix
* Strawberry Alarm Clock
* Sweet Honey in the Rock
* Universal Honey
* Vanilla Fudge
* Vanilla Ice

RANDOM STATS, PART V: POTATOES

6,000: Approximate number of potato growers in the United States.

1.31 million: U.S. acres planted in potatoes in 2002.

446.32 billion: Pounds of potatoes produced in the United States in 2002.

12.02 billion: Pounds of potatoes produced in Idaho in 2001.

5 billion: Pounds of potatoes annually used by Frito-Lay for its Lay's and Ruffles potato chip brands.

134.9: Pounds of potatoes eaten per capita in the U.S. in 2002 (approximately one potato per day, on average).

200: Pounds of potatoes eaten per capita annually in Germany.

5: Pounds of potatoes eaten per capita per day in 19th century Ireland.

$3.15 billion: Value of 2002 U.S. potato production.

54 percent: U.S. consumers who eat potatoes on any given day.

10.75 percent: 2002 per capita potatoes sold in dehydrated form.

12.53 percent: 2002 per capita potatoes sold as chips or shoestrings.

42.25 percent: 2002 per capita potatoes sold as frozen product.

15 months: Shelf life of a can of Pringles brand potato chips.

3 to 4: Potatoes needed to make one standard-sized can of Pringles.

FIVE REGIONAL JAPANESE FAVORITES YOU PROBABLY WON'T FIND IN YOUR LOCAL SUSHI BAR

Even the best local sushi spot caters to the tastes of a mass audience. You'll most likely have to visit Japan to sample these regional specialties:

Battera-zushi. Salted, vinegar-marinated mackerel fillets are pressed between layers of sushi rice and then cut into neat rectangles in this Kansai favorite.

I-zushi. Rice is topped with fermented fish, usually herring, in this specialty of the cold northern climes of Hokkaido province.

Kenshin-zushi. Fresh wild mountain vegetables and herbs top mounds of rice served on bamboo leaves, a springtime favorite in Honshu.

Masu-zushi. In this popular sushi from Toyama Prefecture, small, round cakes of rice and fresh fish are made by wrapping them together in bamboo leaves and then pressing them with a weighted rock in a circular frame.

Ōmura-zushi. In this Kyushu specialty, fresh fish is layered with rice, pressed in a frame, topped with cold omelet, and cut into squares.

THE RHEINHEITSGEBOT

A translation of the 1516 decree by Duke Wilhelm IV of Bavaria, known in English as the German Purity Law, safeguarding beer purity and its sales prices, the first such consumer-protection ordinance:

> We hereby proclaim and decree, by Authority of our Province, that henceforth in the Duchy of Bavaria, in the country as well as in the cities and marketplaces, the following rules apply to the sale of beer:
>
> From Michaelmas to Georgi, the price for one Mass[1] or one Kopf[2] is not to exceed one Pfennig Munich value, and
>
> From Georgi to Michaelmas, the Mass shall not be sold for more than two Pfennigs of the same value, the Kopf not more than three Heller[3].
>
> If this is not adhered to, the punishment stated below shall be administered.
>
> Should any person brew, or otherwise have, other beer than March beer, it is not to be sold any higher than one Pfennig per Mass.
>
> Furthermore, we hereby emphasize that in future in all cities, markets and in the country, the only ingredients used for the brewing of beer must be Barley, Hops and Water. Anyone who knowingly disregards or transgresses upon this ordinance, shall be punished by the confiscation of such barrels of beer, without fail, by Court authorities.
>
> However, should an innkeeper in the country, city or markets buy two or three pails of beer[4] and sell it again to the common peasantry, he alone shall be permitted to charge one Heller more for the Mass of the Kopf, than mentioned above. Furthermore, should there arise a scarcity and subsequent price increase of the barley (also considering that the times of harvest differ, due to location), WE, the Bavarian Duchy, reserve the right to order curtailments for the good of all concerned.

1. Bavarian liter. 2. Head-shaped bowl, slightly smaller than a mass.
3. Half a pfennig. 4. One pail equals 60 mass.

FOOD AND DRINK IN THE BEATLES' *YELLOW SUBMARINE*

For some reason, maybe a major case of the munchies, the Beatles' 1968 animated film *Yellow Submarine* features a feast of visual, spoken, and sung references to food and drink. Here's an exhaustive list, in order of occurrence.

Prologue
* Much of the story takes place in Pepperland.
* Trees in full fruit form a backdrop to a string quartet performance.
* The head Blue Meanie, "Your Blueness," describes Pepperland as "a tickle of joy on the blueberry of the universe."
* Top-hatted Bonkers drop big green apples on Pepperland's citizens.

Opening Credits
* The movie is presented by Apple Films.
* In the song "Yellow Submarine," party sounds with clinking glasses are heard behind the lyric, "And our friends are all aboard."

Liverpool
* During the song "Eleanor Rigby," two prim ladies in a window rapidly eat from two boxes of candy.
* Ringo, trailed by the Yellow Submarine, comments that "It must have been one of them unidentified flying cupcakes."
* In the cavernous interiors of The Pier, a large eggcup holding a soft-boiled egg flies across the hall.
* Ringo and Young Fred enter a room filled with monumental foods on pedestals: a slice of cake, a green pear, a hot dog, a hamburger, a bottle of Fizz cola, and a salami.
* When Frankenstein's monster transforms into John, Ringo scolds him: "I warned you not to eat on an empty stomach."

The Yellow Submarine Sets Sail
* The song "All Together Now" includes the line, "Can I bring my friend to tea?"
* In the Sea of Time, the song "When I'm 64" includes the lines "Birthday greetings, bottle of wine" and "Will you still feed me?"
* The animated 60-second countdown sequence in "When I'm 64" uses an apple and a pear to compose the "8" in "38."

The Sea of Monsters

+ A giant four-legged teakettle pours itself into a walking teacup.
+ The Dreaded Vacuum Flask inhales a three-scoop ice cream cone.
+ While the Beatles search the control panel for the Boxing Button, a giant champagne bottle pops out of the sub and blows its cork.

The Foothills of the Headlands

+ Jeremy Hillary Boob, Ph.D., the "Nowhere Man," repairs one of the submarine's propellers with chewing gum.
+ The song "Lucy in the Sky with Diamonds" mentions "tangerine trees," "marmalade skies," and "marshmallow pies."
+ While the Beatles and Jeremy search for the Sea of Holes, pepper dust on the ground suggests they're close to Pepperland.

Pepperland

+ When love conquers the Blue Meanies, a bluebird of happiness appears holding two maraschino cherries.
+ The song "It's All Too Much" includes the lyric, "All the world is birthday cake, so take a piece but not too much."

DEFENSE FROM THE DAMPS

"Enough," he said; "the cough is a mere nothing; it will not kill me. I shall not die of a cough."

"True—true," I replied; "and, indeed, I had no intention of alarming you unnecessarily—but you should use all proper caution. A draught of this Medoc will defend us from the damps."

Here I knocked off the neck of a bottle which I drew from a long row of its fellows that lay upon the mould.

"Drink," I said, presenting him the wine.

He raised it to his lips with a leer. He paused and nodded to me familiarly, while his bells jingled.

"I drink," he said, "to the buried that repose around us."

"And I to your long life."

*   *   *

The wine sparkled in his eyes and the bells jingled. My own fancy grew warm with the Medoc.

—"The Cask of Amontillado" (1846), Edgar Allan Poe

ADVENTURES IN ICE CREAM, PART II: APRIL FOOL'S FLAVORS

Each April 1, April Fool's Day, enterprising ice cream makers push the boundaries of flavor development. Two of the most newsworthy of such entrepreneurs are Aldrich's Beef & Ice Cream Parlor in Fredonia, New York, and the Tom Wahl's ice cream shops in the Rochester, New York, area, which come up with challenging new one-day flavors every year.

+ Bacon and Eggs[A]
+ Balogna[A]
+ Beef Gravy[A]
+ Beef Hash[A]
+ Beef Stroganoff[A]
+ Cheeseburger[W]
+ Chicken Wing (with blue cheese, hot sauce, celery bits, and real chicken chunks)[A]
+ Chocolate Spaghetti[A]
+ Creamed Corn[A]

+ Dill Pickle[W]
+ Ketchup[W]
+ Minestrone[A]
+ Nacho Cheese[A]
+ Pickles and Cream[A]
+ Pork and Beans[A]
+ Sauerkraut[W/A]
+ Spinach Ripple[A]
+ Succotash (vanilla with lima beans, corn kernels, and pimientos)[A]

A: Aldrich's Beef & Ice Cream Parlor
W: Tom Wahl's

SOME STEAKS NOT NAMED FOR THEIR ANATOMICAL SOURCES

Baseball: Descriptive name for a roughly spherical, two- to three-inch cut of top sirloin, like a large filet mignon. Rich and meaty, it is so thick that it is best cooked no more than medium rare to avoid turning tough.

Butcher's: See *hanger.*

Club: See *Delmonico.*

Chateaubriand: Fancy French name for a thick tenderloin steak, cut close to the filet mignon. The cut is named for a recipe featuring it, in which the steak is grilled with butter and black pepper, created in tribute to the Napoleonic era French diplomat and writer François René, the Viscount of Chateaubriand.

Delmonico: A triangular cut from the short loin, near the rib end, tender and flavorful. The steak is named for the 19th century New York City dining club whose menu featured it.

Flatiron: A tender, flavorful cut from the top shoulder of the chuck section.

Hanger: A hanging muscle, known in French as *onglet*, that wraps around the pancreas and supports the diaphragm. Requiring careful trimming of membrane before cooking, and very flavorful and tender when cooked rare, it is also sometimes known as the "hanging tender" or the "butcher's steak," the latter because the one-per-animal steak was traditionally taken home by meat cutters for their own tables.

Kansas City strip: See *shell.*

New York strip: See *shell.*

Porterhouse: A thick bone-in tenderloin steak, from the sirloin end of the short loin, containing a larger portion of tenderloin than the *T-bone.* Generously sized and very flavorful and rich, the cut is named for the bars in which it was traditionally served, often with a glass of porter or some other robust beer.

Shell: A descriptive name for the flavorful, full-bodied meat that remains after the tenderloin strip is cut away from the short loin. This steak may be served with or without bone.

T-bone: From the center of the short loin, descriptively named for the section of bone that separates its large top loin and smaller tenderloin portions.

TALK OF STRAWBERRIES

Mrs. Elton, in all her apparatus of happiness, her large bonnet and her basket, was very ready to lead the way in gathering, accepting, or talking—strawberries, and only strawberries, could now be thought or spoken of.—"The best fruit in England—every body's favourite—always wholesome.—These the finest beds and finest sorts.—Delightful to gather for one's self—the only way of really enjoying them.—Morning decidedly the best time—never tired—every sort good—hautboy infinitely superior—no comparison—the others hardly eatable—hautboys very scarce—Chili preferred—white wood finest flavour of all—price of strawberries in London—abundance about Bristol—Maple Grove—cultivation—beds when to be renewed—gardeners thinking exactly different—no general rule—gardeners never to be put out of their way—delicious fruit—only too rich to be eaten much of—inferior to cherries—currants more refreshing—only objection to gathering strawberries the stooping—glaring sun—tired to death—could bear it no longer—must go and sit in the shade."

Such, for half an hour, was the conversation.

—*Emma* (1815), Jane Austen

METRIC CONVERSIONS:
FAHRENHEIT TO CELSIUS (CENTIGRADE) AND VICE VERSA

Recipes published in most of the world now use the metric system, which features temperatures given as degrees (°) C. The C stands for one of two interchangeable names applied to the metric temperature scale: Centigrade, literally, "degrees of 100," with 100°C representing the boiling point of water and 0°C its freezing point; or the now more common Celsius, for Swedish scientist and meteorologist Anders Celsius (1701–1744), who first developed this particular measurement scale. The United States and Jamaica still employ the Fahrenheit scale, developed by German physicist and thermometer maker Gabriel Fahrenheit (1686–1736), in which water boils at 212°F and freezes at 32°F.

To convert Fahrenheit temperatures to Celsius,
make the following calculation:
°F − 32 ÷ 1.8 = °C
To convert Celsius temperatures to Fahrenheit,
use the following formula, easily entered on a calculator:
°C × 1.8 + 32 = °F

The following chart allows even quicker conversions for common recipe measurements, with all Celsius temperatures above 65°C rounded to the nearest 5°C to correspond to most gauges. The chart also includes Gas Marks, a simple old British measurement system for oven temperatures found in some older cookbooks; and the even older heat range descriptions.

Fahrenheit	Celsius	Gas Mark	Heat
100°	38°		
105°	40°		
110°	43°		
115°	46°		
120°	49°		
125°	52°		
150°	65°		
175°	80°		
200°	95°		
225°	110°	¼	Very cool

Fahrenheit	Celsius	Gas Mark	Heat
250°	120°	½	
275°	135°	1	Cool
300°	150°	2	
325°	165°	3	Moderate
350°	180°	4	
375°	190°	5	Moderately hot
400°	200°	6	
425°	220°	7	Hot
450°	230°	8	
475°	245°	9	Very hot
500°	260°		
525°	275°		
550°	290°		

RANDOM STATS, PART VI: PASTA

From the National Pasta Association, www.ilovepasta.org:

72 percent: Americans who buy pasta because it tastes good.

64 percent: Americans who buy pasta because it's easy to make.

58 percent: Americans who buy pasta because it's healthy or nutritious.

53 percent: Americans who buy pasta because it's versatile.

48 percent: Americans who buy pasta because it's economical or inexpensive.

43 percent: Americans who buy pasta because the kids love it.

32 percent: Americans who buy pasta because it's fun to eat.

41 percent: Americans who reported having three to five packages of dry pasta in the pantry or cupboard.

33 percent: Americans who reported having one to two packages of dry pasta.

11 percent: Americans who reported having six to seven packages of dry pasta.

11 percent: Americans who reported having eight or more packages of dry pasta.

3 percent: Americans who reported having no dry pasta, or buying it as needed.

2,021,452,000: Gallons of water (equivalent to almost 75,000 Olympic-sized pools) needed to cook one billion pounds of pasta.

SYRUP STAGES, TEMPERATURES, AND TESTS

When making candy and other sweet recipes, sugar and water are often boiled together until they reach a certain point designated by a "stage" name, gauged either by its temperature range or by a physical test. Use a good-quality candy thermometer or, for the physical test, carefully use a spoon to drop some of the syrup into a small bowl of ice water. Never touch the hot syrup before you drop it into the ice water.

Stage	Temperature	Physical Test (after dropping in ice water)
Thread	230–234ºF	Breaks into threads one to two inches long.
Soft ball	234–240ºF	Forms a soft ball when rolled between fingers.
Firm ball	244–248ºF	Forms a firm ball when rolled between fingers.
Hard ball	250–265ºF	Forms a hard ball when rolled between fingers.
Soft crack	270–290ºF	Stretches into flexible strands when pulled.
Hard crack	300–310ºF	Forms a mass that can easily be snapped in two.

Caramels: Boiled to 320–328ºF, syrup reaches the **light caramel** stage, which looks amber when poured onto a heatproof white plate or marble slab. At 350ºF, it reaches the **dark caramel** stage, the familiar caramel color; do not cook it beyond this point, or it will turn unpleasantly bitter.

RANDOM STATS PART VII: AMERICA'S FAVORITE COMFORT FOODS

Rankings in descending order of top-choice preference from a fall 2003 survey by the Food and Brand Lab at the University of Illinois at Urbana-Champaign:

23 percent: Potato chips.
14 percent: Ice cream.
12 percent: Cookies.
11 percent: Chocolate.
11 percent: Pizza or pasta.
9 percent: Steaks and burgers.
9 percent: Casseroles.
7 percent: Soup.
4 percent: Vegetables.
3 percent: Salad.

CHEAT SHEET VIII: SOME JEWISH FOODS

Blintz: Thin egg crepes rolled around a sweetened filling of farmer cheese, pot cheese, or cottage cheese and egg, then baked.

Cholent: A casserole of beans and meat, traditionally cooked in the dying embers of the local bakery's oven during the Sabbath, when Orthodox Jews could not use their home kitchens.

Gefilte fish: Large poached or baked dumplings of pureed whitefish, eggs, matzo meal, onion, and seasonings, usually served cold with grated horseradish.

Kishka: Also known as "stuffed derma," a sausage casing filled with a mixture of barley, flour, onions, chicken fat, and spices, prepared by boiling and then slicing and baking until crisped.

Kugel: A baked pudding usually served as a side dish, based on noodles when sweet or on potato when savory.

Latke: A potato pancake, made by pan-frying or deep-frying a mixture of shredded or grated potato, onion, and flour or matzo meal.

Matzo ball: A large, spherical dumpling served in chicken soup, made from a mixture of matzo meal (ground from Jewish unleavened bread crackers), water, and rendered chicken fat.

THE POWER OF BRANDY

On Wednesday, April 7, I dined with him at Sir Joshua Reynolds's. I have not marked what company was there. Johnson harangued upon the qualities of different liquors; and spoke with great contempt of claret, as so weak, that a man would be drowned by it before it made him drunk. He was persuaded to drink one glass of it, that he might judge, not from recollection, which might be dim, but from immediate sensation. He shook his head, and said, 'Poor stuff! No, Sir, claret is the liquor for boys; port for men; but he who aspires to be a hero (smiling), must drink brandy. In the first place, the flavour of brandy is most grateful to the palate; and then brandy will do soonest for a man what drinking CAN do for him. There are, indeed, few who are able to drink brandy. That is a power rather to be wished for than attained.

—*The Life of Samuel Johnson* (1799), James Boswell

A FATE FIT FOR OYSTERS

'A loaf of bread,' the Walrus said,
'Is what we chiefly need:
Pepper and vinegar besides
Are very good indeed—
Now, if you're ready, Oysters dear,
We can begin to feed.'

'But not on us!' the Oysters cried,
Turning a little blue.
'After such kindness, that would be
A dismal thing to do!'
'The night is fine,' the Walrus said,
'Do you admire the view?'

'It was so kind of you to come!
And you are very nice!'
The Carpenter said nothing but
'Cut us another slice.
I wish you were not quite so deaf
I've had to ask you twice!'

'It seems a shame,' the Walrus said,
'To play them such a trick.
After we've brought them out so far,
And made them trot so quick!'
The Carpenter said nothing but
'The butter's spread too thick!'

'I weep for you,' the Walrus said:
'I deeply sympathize.'
With sobs and tears he sorted out
Those of the largest size,
Holding his pocket-handkerchief
Before his streaming eyes.

'O Oysters,' said the Carpenter,
'You've had a pleasant run!

Shall we be trotting home again?'
But answer came there none—
And this was scarcely odd, because
They'd eaten every one.
—"The Walrus and the Carpenter" from
Through the Looking Glass (1871), Lewis Carroll

ADVENTURES IN ICE CREAM, PART III: THE JAPANESE WAY

A number of different Japanese entrepreneurs are indulging the traditional Japanese taste for exotic and wide-ranging ingredients by incorporating them into ice creams intended not as once-a-year jokes, but as year-round delicacies. These ice cream flavors include

- Abalone
- Cactus
- Cedar Chip
- Cherry Blossom
- Chicken
- Chicken Wing
- Corn
- Crab
- Deep Sea Water
- Eel
- Fried Eggplant
- Garlic (marketed under the "Dracula" brand)
- Goat (both goat's milk and goat meat)
- Horsemeat
- Lettuce-Potato
- Miso (Soybean Paste)
- Natto (fermented soy beans)
- Noodle
- Octopus
- Ox Tongue
- Oyster
- Pickled Orchid
- Pit Viper
- Red Wine
- Rice
- Salmon
- Saury (a local fish)
- Sea Slug
- Sea Urchin
- Seaweed
- Sesame, Soy Bean, and Dried Kelp
- Shark Fin Noodle (with Green Onion and Miso)
- Shochu (potato liquor)
- Short-Necked Clam
- Shrimp
- Silk
- Soft-Shelled Turtle
- Spinach
- Squid
- Stout (black beer)
- Sweet Potato
- Tomato
- Tulip
- Wasabi (green horseradish)
- Whale Meat
- Wheat

THERE NEVER WAS SUCH A CHRISTMAS GOOSE!

Such a bustle ensued that you might have thought a goose the rarest of all birds; a feathered phenomenon, to which a black swan was a matter of course—and in truth it was something very like it in that house. Mrs Cratchit made the gravy (ready beforehand in a little saucepan) hissing hot; Master Peter mashed the potatoes with incredible vigour; Miss Belinda sweetened up the apple-sauce; Martha dusted the hot plates; Bob took Tiny Tim beside him in a tiny corner at the table; the two young Cratchits set chairs for everybody, not forgetting themselves, and mounting guard upon their posts, crammed spoons into their mouths, lest they should shriek for goose before their turn came to be helped. At last the dishes were set on, and grace was said. It was succeeded by a breathless pause, as Mrs Cratchit, looking slowly all along the carving-knife, prepared to plunge it in the breast; but when she did, and when the long expected gush of stuffing issued forth, one murmur of delight arose all round the board, and even Tiny Tim, excited by the two young Cratchits, beat on the table with the handle of his knife, and feebly cried Hurrah!

There never was such a goose. Bob said he didn't believe there ever was such a goose cooked. Its tenderness and flavour, size and cheapness, were the themes of universal admiration. Eked out by apple–sauce and mashed potatoes, it was a sufficient dinner for the whole family; indeed, as Mrs Cratchit said with great delight (surveying one small atom of a bone upon the dish), they hadn't ate it all at last. Yet every one had had enough, and the youngest Cratchits in particular, were steeped in sage and onion to the eyebrows. —*A Christmas Carol* (1843), Charles Dickens

EATING AND DRINKING ACROSS THE MAP, PART VI:
DAIRY DEPARTMENT

Butter Creek Junction, Oregon
Buttermilk, Arkansas (also Kansas)
Buttermilk Falls, Pennsylvania
Buttermilk Shores, Tennessee
Butterville, New York
Cheesetown, Pennsylvania
Cheeseville, Wisconsin

Cream, Wisconsin
Egg Bend, Louisiana
Egg Harbor, Indiana (also Wisconsin)
Egg Harbor City, New Jersey
Egg Lagoon, Tasmania, Australia
Milk Landing, Virginia
Milk Springs, Alabama

CHEAT SHEET IX: SOME GERMAN, EASTERN EUROPEAN, AND RUSSIAN FOODS

Bigos: Polish huntsman's stew of various meats, sausage, sauerkraut, apple, onion, tomato, broth, and Madeira.

Blini: Thin little buckwheat-flour pancakes served in Russia with an earthy, sour flavor. They are drizzled with melted butter and used as a base for caviar, smoked or pickled fish, spreads, or sweet preserves.

Borscht: A Russian soup, either vegetarian or with meat, characterized by abundant vegetables, especially beets.

Chlodnik: A cold, tangy Polish summer vegetable soup.

Dobos torta: Hungary's drum-shaped, chocolate-cream-filled seven-layer cake.

Gulyas: Also known by the more familiar spelling of "goulash," a rustic stew of meat, hot paprika, and caraway seeds, along with onion and potato.

Kugelhopf: An egg-enriched Viennese coffee cake baked in a fluted ring mold of the same name.

Linzertorte: From Linz, Austria, a tart of raspberry jam on a base of almond pastry.

Palacsinta: Sweet, thin pancakes with a variety of fillings.

Paprikash: Eastern European stew of chicken, veal, or pork, generously seasoned with paprika and enriched with sour cream.

Pojarski: Cutlets of chopped veal or chicken, bread crumbs, cream, and seasonings, pan-fried in butter and oil.

Paskha: A rich Russian Easter cheesecake molded into a four-sided pyramid shape and decorated inside and out with almonds and candied fruit.

Pirozhki: Small, crescent-shaped savory pastries filled with meat or fish, onions, cabbage, egg, or mushrooms.

Sachertorte: A chocolate layer cake filled with jam and iced with bittersweet chocolate.

Sauerbraten: Sweet-and-sour pot roast of beef, usually accompanied by dumplings and braised red cabbage with apples.

Spätzle: Literally "little sparrows," tiny dumplings favored in Austria and Germany as an accompaniment for stews.

Wiener schnitzel: Literally a "Viennese cutlet," a broad, thin slice of veal, pork, or beef, coated with bread crumbs and fried in hot fat until golden brown.

PEZ CANDY DISPENSERS

Created in 1927 in Austria by Edward Haas, PEZ candy tablets (a contraction of the German *pfefferminz*), started out as breath mints in tins. The company introduced handy spring-loaded dispensers in 1948 and, in 1952, wishing to expand into the United States and tap into the children's candy market, it added cartoon-style heads to the dispensers (feet were added in 1987). More than three hundred different dispensers in wondrously wide-ranging varieties have now been created, giving rise to a huge collectors' market. Just a few of the recent and current models listed on the company's Web site, www.pez.com:

Bicentennial
Betsy Ross
Daniel Boone
Indian Chief
Indian Squaw
Pilgrim
Uncle Sam
Wounded Soldier

Circus
Clown
Elephant
Horse
Lion
Ringmaster

Crazy Fruits
Orange
Pineapple
Pear

Disney
Baloo
Captain Hook
Dopey
Dumbo
Goofy
Jiminy Cricket
Mary Poppins
Mickey Mouse

Minnie Mouse
Mowgli
Peter Pan
Pinocchio
Snow White
Tinkerbell
Winnie-the-Pooh
Zorro

Eerie Spirits
Diabolic
Scare Wolf
Spook
Vamp
Zombi

Flintstones
Barney Rubble
Dino (Dinosaur)
Fred Flintstone
Pebbles

Garfield
Arlene
Garfield
Garfield Chef
Garfield Pilot
Nermal
Odie
Smiling Garfield

Heroes
Batman
Captain America
Incredible Hulk
Spiderman
Thor
Wolverine

Kooky Zoo
Cockatoo
Giraffe
Moo Moo (Cow)
Panda Bear

Miscellaneous
Annie
Arithmetic
Astronaut
Baseball in Glove
Boy
Bozo
Bullwinkle
Girl
Olive Oyl
Popeye
Psychedelic Eye

Monsters
Creature from the Black
  Lagoon

Frankenstein
Wolfman

Muppets
Fozzie Bear
Gonzo
Kermit the Frog
Miss Piggy

PEZ Bugz
Ant
Bee
Beetle
Centipede
Grasshopper
Ladybug

PEZ Pals
Bride
Doctor
Fireman
Groom
Knight
Mexican Boy
Nurse
Pirate

Policeman
Stewardess

Safari Animals
Crocodile
Elephant
Hippo
Lion

Seasonal
Bunny
Elf
Lamb
Polar Bear
Pumpkin
Reindeer
Santa
Skull
Snowman
Valentine Heart
Witch

Simpsons
Bart
Homer
Lisa

Maggie
Marge

Snoopy and the Peanuts Gang
Charlie Brown
Lucy
Snoopy
Woodstock

Star Wars
C-3P0
Chewbacca
Darth Vader
Luke Skywalker
Princess Leia
R2-D2

Warner Bros Looney Tunes
Bugs Bunny
Daffy Duck
Foghorn Leghorn
Speedy Gonzales
Wile E. Coyote
Yosemite Sam

EATING AND DRINKING ACROSS THE MAP, PART VII: PREPARED DISHES DEPARTMENT

Chili, Illinois (also Indiana, New Mexico, Ohio, and Wisconsin)
Dumpling Creek, Missouri (also North Carolina and Oklahoma)
Dumpling Hill, Nebraska (also Ohio and Vermont)
Dumpling Island, Maine (also Virginia)
Dumpling Mountain, Alaska (also Tennessee)
Flapjack Island, Alaska

Flapjack Lakes, Washington
Hashtown, Indiana
Gravy Branch, Kentucky
Gravy Creek, Oregon
Pancake, Pennsylvania (also Texas and West Virginia)
Sandwich, Illinois (also Maine, New Hampshire, and England)
Soup Creek, California (also Montana and Oregon)
Toast, North Carolina

SOME NATIONAL FOOD OBSERVANCES: SEPTEMBER

Entire month:
> National 5-A-Day Month
> (five servings of fruits or vegetables)
> National Biscuit Month
> National Chicken Month
> National Food Allergy Awareness Month
> National Food Safety Month
> National Honey Month
> National Mushroom Month
> National Organic Harvest Month
> National Papaya Month
> National Potato Month
> National Rice Month

1st: National Cherry Popover Day
4th: National Macadamia Nut Day
5th: National Cheese Pizza Day
8th: National Date Nut Bread Day
11th: National Hot Cross Buns Day
12th: National Chocolate Milkshake Day
14th: National Cream-Filled Donut Day
15th: National Crème de Menthe Day
17th: National Apple Dumpling Day
19th: National Butterscotch Pudding Day
20th: National Punch Day
21st: National Pecan Cookie Day
22nd: National White Chocolate Day
24th: National Cherries Jubilee Day
25th: National Crabmeat Newberg Day
26th: National Food Service Employees Day
National Pancake Day
27th: National Chocolate Milk Day
28th: National Strawberry Cream Pie Day
29th: National Ham Day
National Pumpkin Day
30th: National Mulled Cider Day

CHEAT SHEET X: SOME SPANISH AND PORTUGUESE FOODS

Bacalao: Dried salt cod, soaked in water or milk to reconstitute it, then cooked in one of a wide variety of ways.

Gazpacho: From Andalusia, a cold, thick soup of pureed tomatoes, garlic, sweet red peppers, olive oil, and vinegar, garnished with crisp croutons, chopped egg, onion, cucumber, and other embellishments.

Olla podrida: Literally "putrid pot," but actually a grand Spanish stew of game, sausage, pork, beef, pigs' ears and tails, chicken, and vegetables.

Paella: Spanish short-grain rice simmered with olive oil, saffron, garlic, and onions and such embellishments as seafood, chicken, rabbit, beef, pork, ham or sausage, peas, peppers, tomatoes, and other vegetables.

Tapas: Literally "lids," a term for the dozens of different hot and cold snacks served in Spanish bars. The name comes from the small discs of bread that bartenders placed atop customers' glasses of sherry, to keep dust and flies out.

Tortilla: In Spain, a flat omelet, usually featuring sliced potatoes, which is cut into wedges and may be eaten hot or cold. The dish is not to be confused with the Mexican flatbreads of the same name.

Zarzuela: Traditional Spanish stew of mixed seafood, tomatoes, garlic, onions, peppers, saffron, and white wine.

RANDOM STATS, PART VIII:
GRILLING AND BARBECUING IN THE UNITED STATES

Compiled from recent studies conducted by the Barbecue Industry Association and the Hearth, Patio & Barbecue Association:

76 percent: U.S. households that own a barbecue grill.

1.4: Number of grills owned by the average grill owner.

61 percent: Grill owners who own a liquid propane gas grill.

48 percent: Grill owners who own a charcoal grill.

9 percent: Grill owners who own a natural gas grill.

7 percent: Grill owners who own an outdoor electric grill.

18 percent: Grill owners who have both charcoal and gas grills.

15 percent: Grill owners who barbecue with an indoor grill.

66 percent: Households where men do the grilling.

INGESTIBLE MONUMENTS: SOME FOODS–AND A DRINK–
NAMED FOR FAMOUS PEOPLE

Enterprising chefs, restaurateurs, and food manufacturers have long known that their creations can capture public attention if a famous name is attached to them. Consider:

Baby Ruth: Chocolate-covered nougat, caramel, and peanuts, created by the Curtiss Candy Company in 1921, now owned by Nestlé. Named for President Grover Cleveland's daughter, the first baby ever born in the White House (though many mistakenly think the candy paid tribute to 1920s baseball star George Herman "Babe" Ruth, who indeed at times promoted the product).

Béchamel: Classic creamy French sauce of milk, butter, and flour. Named for its creator, Louis de Béchameil, a 17th century financier and steward to King Louis XIV.

Bellini: Cocktail combining fresh peach juice and the Italian sparkling wine prosecco. Devised at Harry's Bar in Venice and named for the late 15th to early 16th century Venetian painter Giovanni Bellini.

Carpaccio: Italian appetizer of raw prime beefsteak (or sometimes fish), sliced translucently thin, arranged on a fine white china plate with garnishes. Named for Vittore Carpaccio, late 15th to early 16th century Venetian painter whose colors were celebrated for their translucency.

Kung pao: A stir-fry, usually featuring chicken or shrimp, with hot chilies and peanuts. Named for a fabled minister in China's imperial court.

Melba, peach: Syrup-poached peach half with vanilla ice cream and raspberry sauce. Named for late 19th to early 20th century Australian opera star Helen Porter Mitchell, who took the stage name Nellie (the diminutive of Helen) Melba (after her hometown, Melbourne).

Melba toast: Thin, crisp crackers made by slicing already toasted white bread horizontally into two thinner slices, then retoasting. Named for Nellie Melba (see above).

Napoleon: French pastry treat alternating layers of flaky puff pastry and rich custard. Named for the early 19th century French conqueror and emperor.

Parmentier: Any French dish in which potatoes feature prominently. A tribute to the late 18th to early 19th century French agronomist and economist Antoine-Auguste Parmentier, who campaigned to popularize that vegetable.

Pavlova: Crisp meringue shell filled with fruit and whipped cream, the national dessert of Australia and New Zealand. Named for early 20th century Russian ballerina Anna Pavlova, who immortalized the role of the dying swan in *Swan Lake.*

Sandwich: Popular lunchtime meal contained between two slices of bread. Named in 1762 for its English inventor, John Montague, the Fourth Earl of Sandwich, who so loved gambling that he had to find a way to hold his meal in one hand and his cards in the other.

Stroganoff, beef: Thin slices of steak in a sauce of mushrooms, shallots, cognac, and sour cream, served over buttered noodles or rice. Named for Alexander Sergeevich Stroganoff (1733–1811), a Russian nobleman and an intimate friend of Czarina Catherine II.

Wellington, beef: Beef tenderloin covered with pâté, enclosed in puff pastry, and baked. A tribute to Arthur Wellesley, Duke of Wellington, the British general who led the defeat of Napoleon at Waterloo in 1815.

CHAMPAGNE BOTTLE SIZES

Picolo	187.5 ml (1 glass)
Demi or Filette	375 ml (2 glasses)
Bottle	750 ml (8 glasses)
Magnum	1.5 l (16 glasses)
Jeroboam[1]	3 l (32 glasses)
Rehoboam[2]	4.5 l (48 glasses)
Methuselah[3]	6 l (64 glasses)
Salmanazar[4]	9 l (96 glasses)
Balthazar[5]	12 l (128 glasses)
Nebuchadnezzar[6]	15 l (160 glasses)
Melchior[7]	18 l (192 glasses)

1. First king of the 10 tribes of Israel.
2. Son of Solomon, first ruler of the Southern Kingdom of Judah.
3. Hebrew patriarch, lived to age of 969 years.
4. Assyrian emperor in 13th century BC.
5. The third Wise Man who followed the Star of Bethlehem to the Nativity.
6. Babylonian king in the sixth century BC.
7. First of the three Wise Men.

THOREAU ON KITCHEN ECONOMY

The expense of food for eight months, namely, from July 4th to March 1st, the time when these estimates were made—though I lived there more than two years—not counting potatoes, a little green corn, and some peas, which I had raised, nor considering the value of what was on hand at the last date, was

Rice	$ 1.73 ½
Molasses	$ 1.73
(Cheapest form of the saccharine.)	
Rye meal	$ 1.04¾
Indian meal	$ 0.99¾
(Cheaper than rye.)	
Pork	$ 0.22
Flour	$ 0.88
(Costs more than Indian meal, both money and trouble.)	
Sugar	$ 0.80
Lard	$ 0.65
Apples	$ 0.25
Dried apple	$ 0.22
Sweet potatoes	$ 0.10
One pumpkin	$ 0.06
One watermelon	$ 0.02
Salt	$ 0.03

All experiments which failed

Yes, I did eat $8.74, all told; but I should not thus unblushingly publish my guilt, if I did not know that most of my readers were equally guilty with myself, and that their deeds would look no better in print. The next year I sometimes caught a mess of fish for my dinner, and once I went so far as to slaughter a woodchuck which ravaged my bean-field—effect his transmigration, as a Tartar would say—and devour him, partly for experiment's sake; but though it afforded me a momentary enjoyment, notwithstanding a musky flavor, I saw that the longest use would not make that a good practice, however it might seem to have your woodchucks ready dressed by the village butcher.

* * *

Nothing was given me of which I have not rendered some account. It appears from the above estimate, that my food alone cost me in money about twenty-seven cents a week. It was, for nearly two years after this, rye and Indian meal without yeast, potatoes, rice, a very little salt pork, molasses, and salt; and my drink, water. It was fit that I should live on rice, mainly, who love so well the philosophy of India.

* * *

I learned from my two years' experience that it would cost incredibly little trouble to obtain one's necessary food, even in this latitude; that a man may use as simple a diet as the animals, and yet retain health and strength. I have made a satisfactory dinner, satisfactory on several accounts, simply off a dish of purslane (*Portulaca oleracea*) which I gathered in my cornfield, boiled and salted. I give the Latin on account of the savoriness of the trivial name. And pray what more can a reasonable man desire, in peaceful times, in ordinary noons, than a sufficient number of ears of green sweet corn boiled, with the addition of salt? Even the little variety which I used was a yielding to the demands of appetite, and not of health. Yet men have come to such a pass that they frequently starve, not for want of necessaries, but for want of luxuries; and I know a good woman who thinks that her son lost his life because he took to drinking water only.

The reader will perceive that I am treating the subject rather from an economic than a dietetic point of view, and he will not venture to put my abstemiousness to the test unless he has a well-stocked larder.

Bread I at first made of pure Indian meal and salt, genuine hoe-cakes, which I baked before my fire out of doors on a shingle or the end of a stick of timber sawed off in building my house; but it was wont to get smoked and to have a piny flavor, I tried flour also; but have at last found a mixture of rye and Indian meal most convenient and agreeable. In cold weather it was no little amusement to bake several small loaves of this in succession, tending and turning them as carefully as an Egyptian his hatching eggs.

* * *

There is a certain class of unbelievers who sometimes ask me such questions as, if I think that I can live on vegetable food alone; and to strike at the root of the matter at once—for the root is faith—I am accustomed to answer such, that I can live on board nails. If they cannot understand that, they cannot understand much that I have to say.

—*Walden; or, Life in the Woods* (1854), Henry David Thoreau

SOME MILESTONES IN FOOD AND DRINK HISTORY:
17TH CENTURY AD

1606: Apropos of France's peasantry, King Henri IV coins the phrase "a chicken in his pot every Sunday" to describe his desires to conquer poverty in his realm.

1621: The first American Thanksgiving is celebrated by the *Mayflower* Pilgrims and 92 Indian guests in a three-day feast featuring wild game, seafood, breads, plums, wine, and popcorn.

1629: Governor John Endicott plants apple trees in the Massachusetts Bay Colony.

1630: In Japan, the Mogi and Takanashi families found Kikkoman Soy Sauce.

1650: The first English coffeehouse opens in the city of Oxford.

1654: Frenchman Louis de Béchamel invents the creamy white sauce that bears his name as a way of disguising unpalatable salt cod.

1655: Jamaican rum replaces beer in the British Royal Navy.

1657: The East India Company introduces the sale of tea in London.

1666: An apple falling from a tree helps Isaac Newton, a mathematics professor at England's Cambridge University, formulate his law of gravity.

1672: The first coffeehouse opens in Paris.

1675: In an attempt to quell public political discussion in England, King Charles II issues a proclamation to suppress coffeehouses. He revokes it the following year.

1681: Frenchman Denys Papin invents the pressure cooker.

1683: Franz Georg Kolschitzky opens Vienna's first coffeehouse.

1698: Benedictine monk Dom Pierre Pérignon perfects the production of sparkling wine in the French region of Champagne.

SOME CAVIAR TERMS

Beluga: Highly prized large, flavorful roe from the beluga sturgeon, black to dark pearl-gray in color.

Malossol: "Lightly salted," a term designating any highest-grade caviar.

Osetra: Smaller, darker roe from a smaller sturgeon species of the same name.

Payusnaya: Pressed bricks of more heavily salted broken or immature *osetra* or *sevruga* roe.

Sevruga: Dark gray, flavorful roe from the smallest sturgeon species.

EATING AND DRINKING ACROSS THE MAP, PART VIII:
BEVERAGES DEPARTMENT

Cocoa, Florida
Coffee, Georgia (also Virginia)
Coffee Camp, New South Wales, Australia
Coffee Hall, England
Drinkwater Corner, Maine
Lemonade Creek, Wyoming
Lemonade Lake, Wyoming
Lemonade Peak, Idaho
Soda Bay, California
Soda Butte, Wyoming
Soda Hill, North Carolina
Soda Springs, California (also Idaho, Montana, and Texas)
Soda Valley, Arkansas
Sodaville, Oregon
Tea, Missouri (also South Dakota)
Tea Gardens, New South Wales, Australia
Tea Green, England

AN UNLIKELY, LIVELY VICTIM

The first victim was a lively carp brought to the kitchen in a covered basket from which nothing could escape. The fish man who sold me the carp said he had no time to kill, scale or clean it, nor would he tell me with which of these horrible necessities one began. It wasn't difficult to know which was the most repellent. So quickly to the murder and have it over with. On the docks of Puget Sound I had seen fishermen grasp the tail of a huge salmon and lifting it high bring it down on the dock with enough force to kill it. Obviously I was not a fisherman nor was the kitchen table a dock. Should I not dispatch my first victim with a blow on the head from a heavy mallet? After an appraising glance at the lively fish it was evident he would escape attempts aimed at his head. A heavy sharp knife came to my mind as the classic, the perfect choice, so grasping, with my left hand well covered with a dishcloth, for the teeth might be sharp, the lower jaw of the carp, and the knife in my right, I carefully, deliberately found the base of its vertebral column and plunged the knife in it. I let go my grasp and looked to see what had happened. Horror of horrors. The carp was dead, killed, assassinated, murdered in the first, second and third degree. Limp, I fell into a chair, with my hands still unwashed reached for a cigarette, lighted it, and waited for the police to come to take me into custody. After another cigarette my courage returned and I went to prepare poor Mr Carp for the table.

—"Murder in the Kitchen," *The Alice B. Toklas Cookbook* (1953), Alice B. Toklas

SOME FOOD AND DRINK ENTRIES FROM THE DEVIL'S DICTIONARY

American satirist Ambrose Bierce (1842–1914) cast a jaundiced eye on all aspects of life in the dictionary-style entries he wrote as a column from 1881 to 1887 in the *Wasp* magazine. These were compiled and published as *The Devil's Dictionary* in 1911, two years before the writer headed to Mexico to observe and possibly take part in that country's revolution, during which he disappeared and was presumed dead.

Alcohol, *n.* (Arabic *al kohl*, a paint for the eyes.) The essential principle of all such liquids as give a man a black eye.

Bacchus, *n.* A convenient deity invented by the ancients as an excuse for getting drunk.

Brandy, *n.* A cordial composed of one part thunder-and-lightning, one part remorse, two parts bloody murder, one part death-hell-and-the-grave and four parts clarified Satan.

Cabbage, *n.* A familiar kitchen-garden vegetable about as large and wise as a man's head.

Carouse, *v.* To celebrate with appropriate ceremonies the birth of a noble headache.

Connoisseur, *n.* A specialist who knows everything about something and nothing about anything else. An old wine-bibber having been smashed in a railway collision, some wine was pouted on his lips to revive him. "Pauillac, 1873," he murmured and died.

Crayfish, *n.* A small crustacean very much resembling the lobster, but less indigestible.

Dejeuner, *n.* The breakfast of an American who has been in Paris. Variously pronounced.

Dine, *v.* To eat a good dinner in good company, and eat it slow. In dining, as distinguished from mere feeding, the palate and stomach never ask the hand, 'What are you giving us?'

Edible, *adj.* Good to eat, and wholesome to digest, as a worm to a toad, a toad to a snake, a snake to a pig, a pig to a man, and a man to a worm.

Feast, *n.* A festival. A religious celebration usually signalised by gluttony and drunkenness, frequently in honour of some holy person distinguished for abstemiousness.

Glutton, *n.* A person who escapes the evils of moderation by committing dyspepsia.

Hash, *x.* There is no definition for this word—nobody knows what hash is.

Hospitality, *n.* The virtue which induces us to feed and lodge certain persons who are not in need of food and lodging.

Mayonnaise, *n.* One of the sauces which serve the French in place of a state religion.

Nectar, *n.* A drink served at banquets of the Olympian deities. The secret of its preparation is lost, but the modern Kentuckians believe that they come pretty near to a knowledge of its chief ingredient.

Overeat, *v.* To dine.

Pie, *n.* An advance agent of the reaper whose name is Indigestion.

Potable, *adj.* Suitable for drinking. Water is said to be potable; indeed, some declare it our natural beverage, although even they find it palatable only when suffering from the recurrent disorder known as thirst, for which it is a medicine. Upon nothing as has so great and diligent ingenuity been brought to bear in all ages and in all countries, except the most uncivilized, as upon the invention of substitutes for water.

Quaff, *v.* Emptying the 'sparkling wine' down your throat. When it's only whiskey, it's called swallowing.

Rarebit, *n.* A Welsh rabbit, in the speech of the humorless, who point out that it is not a rabbit. To whom it may be solemnly explained that the comestible known as toad-in-a-hole is really not a toad, and that *riz-de-veau a la financière* is not the smile of a calf prepared after the recipe of a she banker.

Rum, *n.* Generically, fiery liquors that produce madness in total abstainers.

Sauce, *n.* The one infallible sign of civilization and enlightenment. A people with no sauces has one thousand vices; a people with one sauce has only nine hundred and ninety-nine. For every sauce invented and accepted a vice is renounced and forgiven.

Tope, *v.* To tipple, booze, swill, soak, guzzle, lush, bib, or swig. In the individual, toping is regarded with disesteem, but toping nations are in the forefront of civilization and power.

Turkey, *n.* A large bird whose flesh when eaten on certain religious anniversaries has the peculiar property of attesting piety and gratitude. Incidentally, it is pretty good eating.

Wheat, *n.* A cereal from which a tolerably good whisky can with some difficulty be made, and which is used also for bread. The French are said to eat more bread *per capita* of population than any other people, which is natural, for only they know how to make the stuff palatable.

FORTUNE COOKIE FORTUNES ON FOOD AND DRINK

The Chinese fortune cookie (*chen eh bing* in Chinese) was actually invented in the United States in the early 20th century. Some credit their creation to Los Angeles-based restaurateur and baker David Jung, who introduced them at his restaurant in that city's Chinatown around 1920; indeed, the city proudly proclaims that the cookie was born there. Others say, however, that it was the brainchild of Japanese designer Makoto Hagiwara for his Japanese teahouse at San Francisco's Panama-Pacific Exhibition in 1915.

Not surprisingly, the little slips of paper inside the twice-folded wafers from time to time refer to food and drink or, even more self-referentially, to Chinese food and fortune cookies.

A good way to keep healthy is to eat more Chinese food.

◆

Alas! The onion you are eating is someone else's water lily.

◆

An empty stomach is not a good political advisor.

◆

Chinese food is fun and healthy.

◆

Don't order pizza when you want Chinese.

◆

Eat healthy. An ounce of prevention is worth a pound of cure.

◆

Fish, rice, fruit, vegetables, and laughter are good for you.

◆

He who has not tasted the bitter does not understand the sweet.

◆

Help! I'm trapped in a fortune cookie factory!

◆

If you are still hungry, have another fortune cookie.

◆

Never be dumb. Eat smart.

◆

Wit is the salt of conversation, not the food.

◆

You have tasted both the bitterness and sweetness of coffee.

You love Chinese food.

◆

You will never know hunger.

RANDOM STATS, PART IX: HOT BEVERAGES

54 percent: Americans who say they drink both traditional and gourmet coffee drinks at different times of day, according to a 2004 survey by the National Coffee Association.

38 percent: Americans who replied the same way in 2003.

4 percent: Americans, according to that 2004 survey, who drink only gourmet coffee drinks.

5 percent: Americans who replied the same way in 2003.

13 percent: American senior citizens who reported enjoying gourmet coffees in the 2004 survey.

9 percent: American seniors who replied the same way in 2003.

80 percent: Approximate number of American adults who are coffee drinkers, according to the 2004 survey.

52 percent: American adults who drink coffee daily, according to that survey.

64 percent: Portion of total United States coffee consumption taken at breakfast.

23 percent: Percentage of the world's 1997 tea production consumed in India, the world's leading consumer.

16 percent: China's 1997 consumption, in second place.

6 percent: 1997 tea consumption in both Russia and the United Kingdom, tied for third.

5 percent: 1997 tea consumption in both Japan and Turkey, tied for fourth.

4 percent: 1997 tea consumption in both Pakistan and the United States, tied for fifth.

3 percent: 1997 tea consumption in both Iran and Egypt, tied for sixth.

1 percent: 1997 tea consumption in Poland, tied for seventh.

0.4 percent: 1997 tea consumption in Australia, in eighth place.

23.6 percent: 1997 tea consumption in the rest of the world.

198.3 percent: Growth of hot chocolate consumption in Japan between 1994 and 1998.

CHEAT SHEET XI: SOME INDIAN FOODS

Bhelpuri: Bombay street snack of crisp puffed rice, toasted lentils, peanuts, onion, cilantro, chick-pea noodles, and sweet chutney.

Biryani: Aromatic long-grained basmati rice simmered with saffron and meat, poultry, seafood, or vegetables, then elaborately garnished to serve as a one-dish meal.

Chapati: Unleavened whole wheat flatbread.

Chutney: A wide range of sweet or savory spicy condiments or relishes.

Dhansak: A Parsee dish of lamb or chicken with a sauce of pureed lentils, vegetables, green chili, cilantro, and crisply fried onions.

Naan: A teardrop-shaped, tangy but mild wheat flatbread baked in the *tandoori* oven.

Papadum: A thin, crisp wafer made from lentil flour, served as an appetizer or accompaniment to main dishes.

Paratha: A multilayered whole wheat flatbread cooked on a griddle.

Raita: A salad or side dish of yogurt and chopped or shredded raw vegetables.

Tandoori: A style of cooking in a bell-shaped clay oven, producing food that is crispy on the outside, juicy within.

Vindaloo: A super-hot, slightly sour curry from southern and western India, flavored with mustard seeds, garlic, vinegar, and tamarind.

SOME UNUSUAL FOOD MUSEUMS

While conventional museums on food-and-drink-related topics may be found all over the world, enthusiasts with a taste for the bizarre can turn up a wide variety of odd, fascinating collections, both in the real world and on the Worldwide Web. Here is a brief sampler.

The Candy Wrapper Museum: This sometimes beautiful, sometimes bizarre, often nostalgia-evoking Internet-based assortment of candy wrapper images features clever, friendly commentary and is amusingly organized into such categories as Big Eats, Critters, Faces, Foreign, Holidaze, and Vices (www.candywrappermuseum.com).

Leavenworth Nutcracker Museum: Located in the charming Bavarian-style town of Leavenworth, Texas, this museum features an ever-growing collection of more than 5,000 nutcrackers, both antique and modern (www.nutcrackermusuem.com).

Lofoten Stockfish Museum: Located in a picturesque barnlike dockside building in Norway's Lofoten Islands, this little museum devotes itself to the history and production of stockfish, better known as salt cod, with exhibits, a video presentation, and edible samples of its namesake ingredient as well as possibly more palatable foods such as waffles and coffee.

The Museum of Burnt Food: Created, founded, and curated by Deborah Henson-Conant, this museum in Arlington, Massachusetts, features a vast array of wittily or ironically titled exhibits, all of which started as real food or drink that, usually through unintentional oversight, became overcooked to the point of charring. Highlights include "Hot Apple Cinder," "King Tut's Tomato," "A Study in Pizza Toast," and "Why, Sure You Can Bake Quiche in a Microwave" (www.burntfoodmuseum.com).

Shin-Yokohama Ramen Museum: Located in the city of Yokohama, Japan, this museum includes vivid displays of instant ramen packaging, exhibits on the manufacture of the popular Japanese soup noodles, and a two-story indoor theme park featuring eight old-fashioned ramen shops from which visitors can purchase and eat different varieties of noodle bowls.

EATING AND DRINKING ACROSS THE MAP, PART IX: SWEETS AND SNACKS DEPARTMENT

Almond, Alabama (also Arkansas, New York, North Carolina, and Wisconsin)
Candy Town, Ohio
Candyland Estates, Tennessee
Chocolate Springs, Texas
Cracker Jack, Pennsylvania
Ice Cream Butte, Montana
Ice Cream Island, Delaware
Ice Cream Slough, Florida
Nutfield, Victoria, Australia (also England)

Nutgrove, Queensland, Australia
Peanut, Arkansas (also California and Pennsylvania)
Popcorn, Indiana
Sorbet Canal, Louisiana
Taffy, Kentucky
Walnut, Arkansas (also California, Illinois, Indiana, Iowa, Kansas, Maryland, Mississippi, and North Carolina)
Walnut Tree, England

THE LUCKY CHARMS

Introduced in 1964, Lucky Charms breakfast cereal from General Mills features colorful marshmallow charms scattered among its oat puffs. Clovers, hearts, moons, and stars were the original four shapes; the others were added later.

Shape	Color
Balloons	Red
Clovers	Green
Hearts	Pink
Horseshoes	Purple
Moons	Yellow*
Pots of gold	Golden
Rainbows	Multicolored
Stars	Orange

*Original color, now blue.

SOME PROPHETIC ANAGRAMS

Discovered with the assistance of www.wordsmith.org/anagram, the following anagrams may be viewed as prophetic nicknames for their subjects.

James Beard (bon vivant, breakfast-loving late dean of American cuisine):
Dabs Jam E'er
◆
Emeril Lagasse (high-energy American TV chef):
Sir Meal As Glee
◆
Jamie Oliver (you-can-do-it British TV chef):
I Jive Morale
◆
Fernand Point (historic French restaurateur/innkeeper):
Patron Fed Inn
◆
Paul Prudhomme (formerly rotund, always jolly New Orleans chef):
A Plumped Humor

RANDOM STATS, PART X: BEER

19: Different versions, depending on market, of Guinness stout.

31 gallons: Volume of a U.S. beer barrel.

1,000,000 barrels: Annual minimum production of a U.S. or Canadian brewery classified as a "large brewery."

15,000 to 1,000,000 barrels: Annual production range of a U.S. or Canadian brewery classified as a "regional brewery."

195,000,000 barrels: Total U.S. beer production in 2001.

22 gallons (83.3 liters): U.S. per capita beer consumption in 2002.

109 liters: Australian per capita beer consumption in 2002.

120 liters: German per capita beer consumption in 2003.

104 liters: British per capita beer consumption in 2003.

17 percent: German adults who think that getting drunk is the goal in drinking beer.

8 percent: British adults who think that getting drunk is the goal in drinking beer.

61 percent: British adults who drink beer (highest percentage in Europe).

82 percent: British men who drink beer (highest percentage in Europe).

92,749 liters: Estimated annual amount of beer lost by absorption in facial hair in Great Britain.

Almost 2,000: Breweries in the United States in 2001.

BREAKFAST AT POOH CORNER

Pooh put the cloth back on the table, and he put a large honey-pot on the cloth, and they sat down to breakfast. And as soon as they sat down, Tigger took a large mouthful of honey . . . and he looked up at the ceiling with his head on one side, and made exploring noises with his tongue, and considering noises, and what-have-we-got-*here* noises . . . and then he said in a very decided voice:

"Tiggers don't like honey."

"Oh!" said Pooh, and tried to make it sound Sad and Regretful. "I thought they liked everything."

"Everything except honey," said Tigger.

Pooh felt rather pleased about this.

—*The House at Pooh Corner* (1928), A. A. Milne

ISLAMIC DUAS (PERSONAL SUPPLICATIONS)

Before a Meal
Bismillahi wa'ala baraka-tillah.
[With Allah's name and upon the blessings granted
by Allah (do we eat).]

After a Meal
Alham do lillah hilla-thee At Amana wa saquana
waja 'alana minal Muslimeen.
[All praise is due to Allah who gave us food and
drink and who made us Muslims.]

OLD-FASHIONED WAYS AND NEWFANGLED UTENSILS

We had pudding before meat; and I thought Mr Holbrook was going to make some apology for his old-fashioned ways, for he began -

"I don't know whether you like newfangled ways."

"Oh, not at all!" said Miss Matty.

"No more do I," said he. "My house-keeper will have these in her new fashion; or else I tell her that, when I was a young man, we used to keep strictly to my father's rule, 'No broth, no ball; no ball, no beef'; and always began dinner with broth. Then we had suet puddings, boiled in the broth with the beef: and then the meat itself. If we did not sup our broth, we had no ball, which we liked a deal better; and the beef came last of all, and only those had it who had done justice to the broth and the ball. Now folks begin with sweet things, and turn their dinners topsy-turvy."

When the ducks and green peas came, we looked at each other in dismay; we had only two-pronged, black-handled forks. It is true the steel was as bright as silver; but what were we to do? Miss Matty picked up her peas, one by one, on the point of the prongs, much as Amine ate her grains of rice after her previous feast with the Ghoul. Miss Pole sighed over her delicate young peas as she left them on one side of her plate untasted, for they would drop between the prongs. I looked at my host: the peas were going wholesale into his capacious mouth, shovelled up by his large round-ended knife. I saw, I imitated, I survived! —*Cranford* (1853), Elizabeth Gaskell

SOME NATIONAL FOOD OBSERVANCES: OCTOBER

Entire month:

National Applejack Month
National Caramel Month
National Chili Month
National Cookie Month
National Dessert Month
National Pasta Month
National Pickled Pepper Month
National Pizza Month
National Popcorn Poppin' Month
National Pork Month
National Pretzel Month
National Seafood Month

3rd: National Caramel Custard Day
5th: National Apple Betty Day
7th: National Frappe Day
8th: National Fluffernutter Day
10th: National Angel Food Cake Day
11th: National Sausage Pizza Day
12th: National Gumbo Day
National World Egg Day
14th: National Dessert Day
17th: National Pasta Day
18th: National Chocolate Cupcake Day
19th: National Seafood Bisque Day
20th: National Brandied Fruit Day
21st: National Pumpkin Cheesecake Day
22nd: National Nut Day
23rd: National Boston Cream Pie Day
24th: National Bologna Day
25th: National Greasy Foods Day
27th: National Potato Day
28th: National Chocolate Day
30th: National Candy Corn Day
31st: National Caramel Apple Day

THE ORIGINS OF MATZOH (UNLEAVENED BREAD)

And Pharaoh rose up in the night, he, and all his servants. . . . And he called for Moses and Aaron by night and said, 'Rise up, get you forth from among my people, both ye and the children of Israel, and go, serve the Lord, as ye have said, and be gone; and bless me also.' And the Egyptians were urgent upon the people, to send them out of the land in haste. . . . And the people took their dough before it was leavened, their kneading troughs being bound up in their clothes upon their shoulders.

*   *   *

And the children of Israel journeyed from Rameses to Succoth, about six hundred thousand men on foot, beside children. And a mixed multitude went up also with them; and flocks and herds, even very much cattle. And they baked unleavened cakes of the dough which they brought forth out of Egypt, for it was not leavened; because they were thrust out of Egypt, and could not tarry, neither had they prepared for themselves any victual.

—Exodus 12:30–39

AS YE FERTILIZE, SO SHALL YE DRINK?

One day, I asked a doctor to explain to me the reason behind wine's power to affect the mood of whomever drinks it in one of four different ways. First, wine may make someone peaceful, benevolent, mild, and kind. Or it might arouse a person to anger, causing him to storm, quarrel, and rage. Third, wine can make a person crudely childish and without shame. Fourth, it can lead a person to fantasy and folly.

"Let me explain it to you," said the doctor. "After the Flood, so wise pagans describe, the first thing Noah began to plant was grapevines. The soil, however, was infertile, so Father Noah smartly fertilized it with manure that he took from animals who had been on the ark: namely, sheep, bears, pigs, and monkeys. Thusly he fertilized his entire vineyard. The resulting wine possessed the natures of those four animals, as it still does to this day. Since God, as philosophy confirms, created all men of four natural elements—air, fire, water, and earth—so will wine affect each person who drinks it according to his particular nature."

—*The Four Wondrous Properties and Effects of Wine* (1553), Georg Merckel

146

FUN WITH FOOD & DRINK, PART V:
HOW TO POUR A POUSSE CAFÉ

A pousse café (French for "coffee shot" or "coffee push") looks like a feat of magic straight out of a Harry Potter book: a narrow, straight-sided glass holding shimmering layer after layer of multicolored liquids, from three to six or more.

In fact, it's simple science, plus a little skill. The scientific aspect is expressed through the liquids' specific gravity—that is, its density relative to water, with water having a baseline specific gravity of 1.00. Denser liquids, generally higher in sugar content and with a specific gravity above that of water, are heavier; less dense liquids, generally with less sugar and more alcohol, are lighter and will tend to float atop heavier ones.

Here's how to compose a pousse café.

1. **Pick your flavors.** Select a complementary combination of colors and flavors from the following list. Make sure the selections have specific gravities that differ by more than a few hundredths of a point, so they'll be less likely to mingle.
2. **Pour carefully, in order.** Skillfully pour each layer not only in meticulous order, from heaviest first to lightest last, but also with a slow, steady hand over the back of a teaspoon with the tip of its bowl held just barely above the top of the previous layer.
3. **Try, try again.** Even if the layers accidentally mingle, as long as the flavors are complementary the results will still be drinkable.

Heaviest (pour first) Specific gravity 1.18
Crème de banane (banana): *golden*
Crème de cassis (black currant): *red*

Specific gravity 1.17
Anisette (anise/licorice): *clear*

Specific gravity 1.16
Grenadine (pomegranate): *orange-red*
Green crème de menthe (mint): *green*

Specific gravity 1.15
Crème de cacao (chocolate): *brown*
Kahlúa (coffee): *dark coffee brown*
White crème de menthe (mint): *clear*

Specific gravity 1.14
Maraschino (cherry): clear
White crème de cacao (chocolate): *clear*

Specific gravity 1.13
Parfait d'amour (rose-orange-vanilla): *violet*

Specific gravity 1.12
Cherry liqueur: *dark red*
Crème de noyaux (almond): *bright red*
Green crème de menthe (mint): *green*
Strawberry liqueur: *pinkish-red*

Specific gravity 1.11
Blue curaçao (orange): *blue*
Galliano (vanilla-orange): *amber*

Specific gravity 1.10
Amaretto (almond): *amber*
Blackberry liqueur : *dark red*
Orange curaçao (orange): *orange*

Specific gravity 1.09
Apricot liqueur: *orange*
Cranberry liqueur: *cranberry red*
Tia Maria (coffee-rum): *coffee brown*
Triple Sec (orange): *clear*

Specific gravity 1.08
Drambuie (whisky-honey-herbs): *reddish amber*
Frangelico (hazelnut): *brown*
Sambuca (anise/licorice): *clear*

Specific gravity 1.07
Apricot brandy: *amber*
Blackberry brandy: *purple-red*
Campari (bitter herb-fruit-spice): *red*

Specific gravity 1.06
Cherry brandy: *purple-red*
Peach brandy: *yellow-orange*
Yellow Chartreuse (herbal): *neon yellow*

Specific gravity 1.05
Midori (melon): *bright lime green*
Kümmel (sweet caraway): *clear*
Peach schnapps: *clear*
Rock and rye (rye whiskey-citrus): *amber*

Specific gravity 1.04
Sloe gin (blackthorn plum): *purple-red*
Bénédictine & Brandy (herbal-brandy): *amber*
Brandy: *amber*
Cointreau (orange peel): *clear*
Peppermint schnapps: *clear*

Specific gravity 1.01
Green Chartreuse (herbal): *green*

Specific gravity 1.00
Water

Specific gravity 0.98
Tuaca (brandy-vanilla-orange): *amber*

Specific gravity 0.97
Southern Comfort (bourbon-fruit): *amber-orange*

Lightest (pour last) Specific gravity 0.94
Kirsch (cherry): *clear*

RECOMMENDED REFRIGERATOR OR FREEZER FOOD STORAGE TIMES

Use the following suggested storage times only as basic guidelines, letting common sense—and your senses of sight and smell—be the leading indicators of when you should toss food. When in doubt, always err on the side of caution. Be sure to wrap food properly and to refrigerate or freeze it as early as possible. Place perishables in the refrigerator as soon as you return home from shopping (you may want to place perishables in a cooler in your car for the trip home), and do not leave leftovers standing at room temperature longer than absolutely necessary. When refrigerator or freezer storage times are not given below for a particular item, that means they should not be stored in that way.

Food	Refrigerator	Freezer
Dairy		
Butter or margarine	2 weeks	9 months
Buttermilk	1 to 2 weeks	
Cheese, Parmesan, grated	6 to 12 weeks	6 to 12 months
Cheese, hard, whole or sliced	2 to 4 weeks	6 to 12 months
Cheese, soft spreads	3 to 4 weeks	
Cottage cheese	7 days (after "sell by" date)	
Cream, unwhipped	10 days	
Cream, whipped	1 day	2 months
Ice cream		2 months
Milk, canned, opened	3 to 5 days	
Milk, fresh	5 to 7 days	
Sour cream	4 weeks	
Yogurt	7 days (after "sell by" date)	
Eggs		
Fresh, in the shell	3 weeks	
Hard-boiled	1 week	
Meats and Poultry, Raw		
Beef steaks and roasts	3 to 5 days	6 to 12 months
Chicken or turkey, pieces	1 to 2 days	9 to 12 months
Chicken or turkey, whole	1 to 2 days	1 year
Duck or goose, whole	1 to 2 days	6 months

Food	Refrigerator	Freezer
Giblets	1 to 2 days	3 to 4 months
Ground meat or stew meat	1 to 2 days	3 to 4 months
Lamb, roasts or chops	3 to 5 days	6 to 9 months
Pork, roasts or chops	3 to 5 days	4 to 6 months
Prestuffed pork or lamb chops or chicken breasts	1 day	
Sausage	1 to 2 days	1 to 2 months
Variety meats	1 to 2 days	3 to 4 months
Meats, Cooked		
Ham, half, fully cooked	3 to 5 days	1 to 2 months
Ham, slices, fully cooked	3 to 4 days	1 to 2 months
Ham, whole, fully cooked	7 days	1 to 2 months
Hot dogs, cold cuts, and luncheon meats, opened	3 to 7 days	1 to 2 months
Hot dogs and luncheon meats, unopened	2 weeks	1 to 2 months
Leftover broth or gravy	1 to 2 days	2 to 3 months
Leftover cooked meat	3 to 4 days	2 to 3 months
Leftover cooked poultry	3 to 4 days	4 to 6 months
Leftover fried chicken nuggets, tenders, or patties	1 to 2 days	1 to 3 months
Pork sausage, breakfast	7 days	1 to 2 months
Seafood, Raw		
Clams and mussels, live	2 to 3 days	
Clams and mussels, shucked	1 to 2 days	3 to 4 months
Crab and lobster, live	same day	
Crabmeat or shrimp	2 to 3 days	4 months
Fatty fish (such as bluefish, mackerel, mullet, salmon, swordfish, tuna)	1 to 2 days	2 to 3 months
Lean fish (such as cod, flounder, haddock, halibut, perch, trout)	1 to 2 days	4 to 6 months
Oysters, live	7 to 10 days	
Oysters, shucked	5 to 7 days	3 to 4 months
Scallops	2 to 3 days	3 months

Food	Refrigerator	Freezer
Cooked Fish		
Fish, cooked from fresh	3 to 4 days	3 months
Fish sticks		18 months
Shrimp, breaded, packaged		1 year
Tuna salad, prepared	2 to 3 days	
Fruits, Fresh Whole		
Apples	1 month	
Avocados	3 to 5 days	
Berries	2 to 3 days	
Cherries	2 to 3 days	
Citrus fruit	2 weeks	
Grapes	3 to 5 days	
Guavas, mangoes, papayas	1 to 2 days	
Kiwis	3 to 5 days	
Melons	1 week	
Pears	3 to 5 days	
Pineapples	2 to 3 days	
Stone fruit (such as apricots, peaches, plums)	3 to 5 days	
Vegetables, Fresh Whole		
Artichokes	1 week	
Asparagus	2 to 3 days	
Beets, carrots	2 weeks	
Beans, broccoli, lima beans, peas, summer squashes	3 to 5 days	
Cauliflower	1 week	
Cilantro, parsley	2 to 3 days	
Corn	Same day	
Green onions	3 to 5 days	
Celery, cabbage, chilies, green beans, peppers, tomatoes	1 week	
Greens: chards, collard, kale, mustard, spinach	3 to 5 days	
Lettuce and salad greens	1 week	

Food	Refrigerator	Freezer
Mushrooms, okra	1 to 2 days	
Radishes	2 weeks	

Baked Goods
Breads

Food	Refrigerator	Freezer
Breads, yeast		6 to 12 months
Muffins, rolls, quick breads		2 to 4 months
Pancakes and waffles, frozen		1 to 2 months

Cookies

Food	Refrigerator	Freezer
Baked		4 to 6 months
Unbaked dough	2 to 3 days	6 months

Cakes

Food	Refrigerator	Freezer
Angel and sponge cake		4 to 6 months
Cheesecake	3 to 7 days	4 to 6 months
Fruitcake		1 year
Layer cake		6 months

Pastries

Food	Refrigerator	Freezer
Danish		3 months
Doughnuts		3 months

Pies

Food	Refrigerator	Freezer
Chiffon, cream, or pumpkin pie	1 to 2 days	1 month
Fruit pie, baked	1 to 2 days	1 year
Fruit pie, unbaked		8 months

THE SIGN OF CIVILISATION

We may live without poetry, music and art;
We may live without conscience, and live without heart;
We may live without friends; we may live without books;
But civilised man cannot live without cooks.
He may live without books,—what is knowledge but grieving?
He may live without hope—what is hope but deceiving?
He may live without love,—what is passion but pining?
But where is the man that can live without dining?
—*Lucile* (1860), Edward Bulwer-Lytton

SOME FEARFUL FOODS

On the NBC television show *Fear Factor,* a reality show in which contestants compete in various daunting tasks that challenge common fears, participants have been subjected to eating a wide range of gross but generally harmless, sometimes even nutritious, foods.

Creepy-Crawlies
Beetles, stink
Cockroaches, Madagascar hissing
Crickets
Dragonflies
Grasshoppers
Maggots
Slugs
Snails, live
Spiders, African cave-dwelling
Worm "juice"
Worms, nightcrawler
Worms, red
Worms, silk
Worms, tomato horn

Innards
Bile, cow
Blood, cows, coagulated
Brains, cow
Brains, calf
Ears, pig
Eyes, cow
Eyes, sheep
Heart, pig
Intestines, cow
Intestines, pig
Kidney, pig
Liver, pig
Rectum, horse
Rectum, pig
Snout, bull
Snout, pig

Spinal cord, bull
Spleen, bull
Spleen, cow
Stomach, cow
Stomach, pig
Testicles, buffalo
Testicles, reindeer
Tongue, duck
Tongue, pig
Uterus, pig

From the Sea
Cod egg sacs, ant-covered
Cod liver
Cod liver oil
Cod sperm
Fish eyes
Fish sauce, fermented
Squid, fly-covered
Squid guts, fermented

Miscellaneous
Balut (Philippine duck egg with embryo)
Cheese, rancid
Chilies, habanero
Durian (powerfully smelly Asian fruit)
Egg, hundred-year-old
Egg, ostrich, raw
Milk, goat's, drunk directly from the goat

SOME MILESTONES IN FOOD AND DRINK HISTORY:
18TH CENTURY AD

1707: Famed English food shop Fortnum and Mason opens on Piccadilly in London.

1709: German physicist Gabriel Fahrenheit introduces a thermometer on which the boiling point of water is marked at 212°.

1720: The famed Caffè Florian opens in Venice, Italy.

1727: Coffee growing begins in Brazil, now the world's largest producer.

1736: England's Parliament passes the Gin Act to ban that liquor's public sale in London. The act is repealed six years later.

1740: Booth's gin distillery established in London.

1743: In Epernay, France, Claude Moët founds the Champagne business that will become Moët et Chandon.

1744: First written account of ice cream in America, in the colony of Maryland.

1747: Hannah Glasse publishes *The Art of Cookery*, the first great English cookbook.

1756: France's duc de Richelieu devises a rich, thick sauce made by emulsifying egg yolks and olive oil, naming it "Mahonnaise" after Mahón, a British fort his forces captured in the Seven Years' War.

1759: Arthur Guinness establishes a brewery in Dublin, Ireland.

1762: England's John Montague, Earl of Sandwich, comes up with a tidy way to eat a meal while at the gambling tables, by holding meat between two slices of bread.

1773: Protesting British tea taxes, Bostonians including Paul Revere disguise themselves as Indians, surreptitiously board three East India Company ships in Boston's harbor, and dump 342 chests of tea into the water in an act that comes to be known as the Boston Tea Party. Coffee becomes America's preferred hot beverage.

1777: In Dijon, France, Maurice Grey develops Grey Poupon mustard.

1786: Scottish poet Robert Burns completes his "Address to a Haggis" (see page 106–107).

1795: In Kentucky, Jacob Beam founds the bourbon-distilling company that will come to be known as James B. Beam Distilling Co., makers of Jim Beam.

CHEAT SHEET XII: SOME FRENCH FOODS

Aïoli: Provençal garlic mayonnaise served as a dip, a condiment, or an embellishment for seafood soups and other hot dishes.

Ballotine: Boned poultry, meat, or seafood, flattened, stuffed, rolled, cooked in a flavorful liquid, then sliced and served hot with a sauce based on the liquid.

Basquaise: Basque-style garnish for a main dish, featuring ham, meaty-tasting mushrooms called *cèpes*, and potato.

Bavarois: "Bavarian" dessert of flavored custard, gelatin, and whipped cream.

Béarnaise: Classic sauce for steak and other meats, made by beating together egg yolks, melted butter, white wine, vinegar, shallots, and tarragon.

Béchamel: Classic sauce based on milk, thickened with the butter-flour paste called *roux*, used on its own, as a binder for fillings or stuffings, or as the base for cheese sauces or other sauces.

Beurre blanc: "White butter" sauce made by cooking minced shallots in vinegar, then whisking in butter cubes to make a thick, foamy emulsion.

Blancmange: Molded gelatin dessert based on milk, ground almonds, and whipped cream.

Blanquette: Veal, chicken, or lamb cooked with pearl onions, baby mushrooms, and a velouté sauce enriched with egg yolks and cream.

Bordelaise: Bordeaux-style sauce for grilled meat, made from red wine, the concentrated veal stock known as *demi-glace*, shallots, and fresh herbs.

Bouillabaisse: The main course fish soup of Marseilles, abounding in whitefish, eel, shellfish, shrimp, and sometimes lobster; cooked with white wine, tomatoes, olive oil, garlic, onions, and such signature seasonings of Provence as fennel, saffron, and dried orange peel.

Bourguignonne: A Burgundy-style braise, usually of beef, with red wine, mushrooms, pearl onions, and bacon or salt pork.

Brioche: Large or small yeast-leavened breads made from a dough so laden with eggs and butter that it almost approaches cake. (In fact, the famed quote "Let them eat cake," attributed to Marie-Antoinette, the wife of King Louis XVI, when she was told the peasants had no bread, was actually, "Let them eat brioche.")

Cassoulet: From the Languedoc, a slowly baked stew of white beans, lamb, pork, sausage, and preserved goose.

Choucroute: Alsatian main course of sauerkraut slowly simmered with sausages and other cured meats.

Clafoutis: Batter-based fresh fruit pudding from the Limousin region.

Coq au vin: Chicken stewed in red wine with bacon, pearl onions, and carrots.

Daube: A slow braise of beef, lamb, pork, or goose, cooked with aromatic vegetables, pork rinds, and salt pork.

Dijonnaise: Sauced or seasoned with the signature mustard of Dijon.

Florentine: Refers to a dish served Florence-style, with spinach.

Foie gras: The buttery liver of specially fattened geese or ducks, usually served sliced and quickly sautéed or as part of a pâté.

Garbure: Traditional Béarnaise stew of vegetables and preserved meat.

Génoise: Light yet buttery sponge cake.

Gougère: Crisp baked cheese-flavored pastry puffs.

Grecque: "Greek" style of cooking vegetables with white wine, vinegar, olive oil, lemon juice, herbs, and spices.

Hollandaise: A rich warm sauce made with butter, eggs, and lemon juice.

Lyonnaise: Cooked with onions, in the style of Lyons.

Marchand de vin: In the style of a "wine merchant," usually referring to steak with a sauce of red wine, stock, shallots, butter, lemon, and parsley.

Meunière: In the style of the "miller's wife," usually applied to sole dusted with flour, salt, and pepper, sautéed in butter, and finished with lemon and parsley.

Mille-feuille: A "thousand-leaf" pastry made from sheets of flaky puff pastry dough interspersed with a creamy filling.

Mornay: A *béchamel* enriched with grated cheese, served with fish, chicken, eggs, or vegetables.

Niçoise: In the style of the city of Nice, in Provence, characterized by such local ingredients as tomatoes, garlic, olives, olive oil, and anchovies.

Parmentier: Featuring potatoes, named in honor of France's late 18th to early 19th century champion of the tubers, Antoine-Auguste Parmentier.

Périgourdine: In the style of Perigord, featuring that region's black truffles.

Pipérade: A Basque specialty of peppers, pimientos, tomatoes, onions, and garlic, fried together and then mixed with eggs to make a soft omelet.

Pot-au-feu: A "pot on the fire," referring to meats and vegetables slowly simmered together in broth to make a main dish.

Poule au pot: Literally "chicken in the pot," a whole chicken poached with vegetables in rich broth.

Printanière: "Springtime-style," referring to any dish generously garnished with tender spring vegetables.

Ratatouille: Provence's vegetable stew of eggplant, zucchini, peppers, onions, garlic, olive oil, and herbs.

BEN FRANKLIN ON HOW TO MAKE WINE

Friendly READER,

Because I would have every Man make Advantage of the Blessings of Providence, and few are acquainted with the Method of making Wine of the Grapes which grow wild in our Woods, I do here present them with a few easy Directions, drawn from some Years Experience, which, if they will follow, they may furnish themselves with a wholesome sprightly Claret, which will keep for several Years, and is not inferior to that which passeth for French Claret.

Begin to gather Grapes from the 10th of September (the ripest first) to the last of October, and having clear'd them of Spider webs, and dead Leaves, put them into a large Molosses- or Rum-Hogshead; after having washed it well, and knock'd one Head out, fix it upon the other Head, on a Stand, or Blocks in the Cellar, if you have any, if not, in the warmest Part of the House, about 2 Feet from the Ground; as the Grapes sink, put up more, for 3 or 4 Days; after which, get into the Hogshead bare-leg'd, and tread them down until the Juice works up about your Legs, which will be in less than half an Hour; then get out, and turn the Bottom ones up, and tread them again, a Quarter of an Hour; this will be sufficient to get out the good Juice; more pressing wou'd burst the unripe Fruit, and give it an ill Taste: This done, cover the Hogshead close with a thick Blanket, and if you have no Cellar, and the Weather proves Cold, with two.

In this Manner you must let it take its first Ferment, for 4 or 5 Days it will work furiously; when the Ferment abates, which you will know by its making less Noise, make a Spile-hole within six Inches of the Bottom, and twice a Day draw some in a Glass. When it looks as clear as Rockwater, draw it off into a clean, rather than new Cask, proportioning it to the Contents of the Hogshead or Wine (*1) Vat; that is, if the Hogshead holds twenty Bushels of Grapes, Stems and all, the Cask must at least, hold 20 Gallons, for they will yield a Gallon per Bushel. Your Juice or (*2) Must thus drawn from the Vat, proceed to the second Ferment.

You must reserve in Jugs or Bottles, 1 Gallon or 5 Quarts of the Must to every 20 Gallons you have to work; which you will use according to the following Directions.

Place your Cask, which must be chock full, with the Bung up, and open twice every Day, Morning and Night; feed your Cask with the reserved Must; two Spoonfuls at a time will suffice, clearing the Bung after you feed it, with your Finger or a Spoon, of the Grape-Stones and other Filth which the Ferment will throw up; you must continue feeding it thus until Christmas, when you may bung it up, and it will be fit for Use or to be rack'd into clean Casks or Bottles, by February.

N. B. Gather the Grapes after the Dew is off, and in all dry Seasons. Let not the Children come at the Must, it will scour them severely. If you make Wine for Sale, or to go beyond Sea, one quarter Part must be distill'd, and the Brandy put into the three Quarters remaining. One Bushel of Grapes, heap Measure, as you gather them from the Vine, will make at least a Gallon of Wine, if good, five Quarts.

These Directions are not design'd for those who are skill'd in making Wine, but for those who have hitherto had no Acquaintance with that Art.

(*1) Vat or Fatt, a Name for the Vessel, in which you tread the Grapes, and in which the Must takes its first Ferment.

(*2) Must is a Name for the Juice of the Vine before it is fermented, afterwards 'tis called Wine.

—*Poor Richard: An Almanack* (1743)

CHEAT SHEET XIII: SOME SCANDINAVIAN FOODS

Frikadeller: Sautéed Danish meatballs combining veal, pork, bread crumbs, onion, egg, milk, and seasonings.

Gravlax: Literally "buried salmon," raw fillets cured by layering them with fresh dill, sugar, salt, and pepper, then weighing them down for several days.

Rødgrød med fløded: "Red gruel with cream," a popular dessert of pureed raspberries and currants thickened with arrowroot and chilled, then served with chilled cream.

Smørrebrød: Literally "buttered bread," referring to a wide variety of traditional Danish open-faced sandwiches.

SOME NATIONAL FOOD OBSERVANCES: NOVEMBER

Entire month:

    National Fun with Fondue Month

    National Georgia Pecan Month

    National Peanut Butter Lovers Month

1st–7th: National Fig Week

2nd: National Deviled Egg Day

3rd: National Sandwich Day

4th: National Candy Day

    National Men Make Dinner Day

5th: National Doughnut Day

6th: National Nachos Day

7th: National Bittersweet Chocolate with Almonds Day

8th: National Cook Something Bold and Pungent Day

10th: National Vanilla Cupcake Day

12th: National Pizza with the Works Except Anchovies Day

13th: National Indian Pudding Day

15th: National Clean Out Your Refrigerator Day

17th: National Baklava Day

20th: National Peanut Butter Fudge Day

23rd: National Cashew Day

24th: National Espresso Day

25th: National Parfait Day

26th: National Cake Day

27th: National Bavarian Cream Pie Day

28th: National French Toast Day

29th: National Chocolates Day

30th: National Mousse Day

MAKING HOLIDAY FRUIT CAKES

Eggbeaters whirl, spoons spin round in bowls of butter and sugar, vanilla sweetens the air, ginger spices it; melting, nose-tingling odors saturate the kitchen, suffuse the house, drift out to the world on puffs of chimney smoke. In four days our work is done. Thirty-one cakes, dampened with whiskey, bask on windowsills and shelves.

—"A Christmas Memory" (1966), Truman Capote

FIVE GOOD REASONS

If on my theme I rightly think,
There are five reasons we should drink,—
Good wine, a friend, because we're dry,
Or lest we should be by and by,
Or any other reason why.
                    —Jean Sirmond (app. 1589–1649)

RANDOM STATS, PART XI: PIZZA

---

100 acres: Approximate amount of pizza eaten daily in the United States.

350: Slices of pizza eaten every second, on average, in the United States.

17 percent: Portion of all U.S. restaurants that are pizzerias.

93 percent: Americans who eat pizza at least once a month.

42 percent: American children between 6 and 11 years old who eat pizza within any given three-day period.

62 percent: Americans who prefer pizza topped with meat.

38 percent: Americans who prefer pizza topped with vegetables.

36 percent: Pizza orders featuring pepperoni, favorite topping in the United States.

3 billion: Approximate number of pizzas sold annually in the United States.

2.5 billion-plus: Approximate number of pizzas eaten annually in Italy.

7,500 tons: Amount of olive oil used annually in Italy to make pizzas.

90,000 tons: Mozzarella cheese used annually in Italy to make pizzas.

45,000 tons: Tomatoes used annually in Italy to make pizzas.

135,000 tons: Flour used annually in Italy to make pizzas.

$2,782,254,592: Total 2003 U.S. sales of top 10 frozen pizza brands in the United States (in descending order: DiGiorno, Tombstone, Red Baron, Freschetta, store brands, Totino's Party Pizza, Tony's, Stouffer's, Jack's, and Celeste).

VALOR ON THE HALF-SHELL

He was a very valiant man who first adventured on eating of oysters.
                    —*The History of the Worthies of England* (1662), Thomas Fuller

SOME MILESTONES IN FOOD AND DRINK HISTORY:
19TH CENTURY AD

1801: Jonathan Chapman of Massachusetts begins over four decades roaming the territories that would become Ohio, Indiana, and Illinois, planting seeds of the apple trees he loves, entering legend as "Johnny Appleseed."

1803: Maryland farmer Thomas Moore invents an insulated icebox.

1805: At Mission San Gabriel, near Los Angeles, Spanish friars plant the first California orange grove.

1823: English miller Jeremiah Colman begins making powdered mustard.

1824: John Cadbury opens a tea and coffee shop in Birmingham, England, where he also begins developing chocolate products.

1825: Frenchman Jean-Anthelme Brillat-Savarin publishes a landmark book on food and drink, *La Physiologie du Goût* (*The Physiology of Taste*). Both author and book are best known to food lovers through the centuries for his statement: "Tell me what you eat and I will tell you what you are," generally digested to the more succinct, "You are what you eat."

1828: Dutch chocolatier Conrad van Houten develops powdered cocoa.

1832: In Vienna, baking apprentice Franz Sacher makes a jam-filled chocolate cake, the Sachertorte, in tribute to Prince Klemens von Metternich.

1837: Brothers-in-law William Procter and James Gamble form Procter and Gamble in Cincinnati.

1852: Hungarian Count Agoston Haraszthy plants varietal grapevines in Sonoma County, California, giving birth to that state's wine industry.

1855: A commission appointed by Napoleon III officially ranks France's greatest vineyards, including Château Haut-Brion, Château Lafitte-Rothschild, Château Latour, Château Margaux, and Château d'Yquem.

1856: Joseph Schlitz founds a brewery in Milwaukee, Wisconsin.

1858: John Landis Mason patents his Mason jar, especially designed for canning and preserving, in New York.

1860: French chemist Louis Pasteur develops pasteurization as a way to sterilize milk by heating it to 125°C (257°F), the point at which bacteria die.

1863: President Lincoln declares Thanksgiving an official U.S. holiday.

1866: Tennessean Jack Daniel launches his sour mash whiskey in Lynchburg.

1867: Baked Alaska is introduced at Delmonico's restaurant in New York as a tribute to the U.S. purchase of the Alaskan Territory.

1868: Edmund McIlhenny develops Tabasco hot pepper sauce on Avery Island in Louisiana.

1869: Husband and wife John and Mary Ann Sainsbury open a dairy shop in London, which will grow into Britain's premier supermarket chain.

1869: In Camden, New Jersey, Joseph Campbell and Abram Anderson establish a vegetable cannery that will grow into the Campbell Soup Company.

1869: Henry John Heinz enters the packaged food business in Sharpsburg, Pennsylvania, by processing bottled horseradish.

1871: The Pillsbury family founds its namesake flour-milling company in Minneapolis, Minnesota.

1873: Adolph Coors and Jacob Schueler found a brewery in the Colorado Territory town of Golden.

1874: While demonstrating a soda fountain in Philadelphia, Robert Green adds a scoop of ice cream to a mixture of carbonated water and syrup, creating the first ice cream soda.

1875: The first milk chocolate is developed in Vevey, Switzerland.

1876: Heinz introduces its brand of bottled tomato ketchup.

1877: In Battle Creek, Michigan, surgeon and vegetarian John Harvey Kellogg develops and markets a breakfast cereal of wheat, oats, and cornmeal, which he calls Granula, changing the name to Granola four years later.

1883: Oscar Mayer begins selling wieners at his Chicago butcher shop.

1886: Famed gourmet grocery Fauchon opens in Paris.

1886: In Lancaster, Pennsylvania, Milton Snavely Hershey goes into business making caramels, soon to branch out into chocolate.

1886: Atlanta pharmacist John Pemberton develops a syrup, to be mixed with carbonated water, which he describes as an "esteemed Brain tonic and Intellectual Beverage," marketing it under the name of Coca-Cola.

1890: Scottish grocer Thomas Lipton begins packaging and selling tea.

1892: William Painter develops the crown bottle cap in Baltimore, Maryland.

1892: The New York Biscuit Co., which in 1898 will merge with three other companies to become National Biscuit Co. (Nabisco), launches a fig jam–filled soft cookie, naming it after the Boston suburb of Newton.

1894: Iceberg lettuce is introduced to gardeners by the Burpee seed company.

1895: The first U.S. pizzeria opens in New York City.

1896: Fannie Farmer publishes her famed *Boston Cooking School Cookbook.*

1896: A salesman for Chicago confectioner brothers F. W. and Louis Rueckheim comes up with a name for their caramel-coated popcorn with peanuts when he tastes it and says, "That's a crackerjack!"

1900: Milton Hershey sells his first chocolate bars.

1900: A systematic restaurant guidebook is published for the first time with the launch of the *Guide Michelin* in Paris.

CHEKHOV ON VODKA

The Russian national spirit figures prominently in the works of author and playwright Anton Chekhov (1860–1904), including the following:

> To tell the truth, all our family have a great taste for vodka.
> —"An Adventure"

♦

> "That's why you have no idea of singing—because you care more for vodka than for godliness, you fool." —"Choristers"

♦

> "Why do you keep on with tea and nothing but tea? You should have a drop of vodka!" —"The Cook's Wedding"

♦

> I am not at all surprised that in the new works with which our literature has been enriched during the last ten or fifteen years the heroes drink too much vodka and the heroines are not over-chaste.
> —"A Dreary Story"

♦

> They began by drinking a big wine-glass of vodka and eating oysters. —"Drunk"

♦

> A cut-glass decanter of vodka, which diffused a smell of orange peel all over the room when it was poured out, was put on the table also. —"The Horse Stealers"

♦

> Petty feelings of envy, vexation, wounded vanity, of that small, provincial misanthropy engendered in petty officials by vodka and a sedentary life, swarmed in his heart like mice. —"The Husband"

♦

> It seemed to him as though, instead of vodka, he had swallowed dynamite, which blew up his body, the house, and the whole street.
> —"An Inadvertence"

♦

> Do I smell of vodka? How strange! And yet, it is not so strange after all. I met the magistrate on the road, and I must admit that we did drink about eight glasses together. —*Ivanoff*

♦

He came at dinner-time, dined with them and stayed a very long
time. That would not have mattered. But they had to buy vodka,
which Groholsky could not endure, for his dinner. He would drink
five glasses and talk the whole dinner-time. —"A Living Chattel"

♦

At that season he would have to take longer walks about the
garden and beside the river, so as to get thoroughly chilled, and then
drink a big glass of vodka and eat a salted mushroom or a soused
cucumber, and then—drink another. —"The Lottery Ticket"

♦

There was a warmth inside him from the vodka.
He looked with softened feelings at his friends, admired them
and envied them. —"A Nervous Breakdown"

♦

Sitting down to dinner, Somov, who is fond of good eating and
of eating in peace, drinks a large glass of vodka and begins
talking about something else. —"A Pink Stocking"

♦

After a cigar or a glass of vodka . . . your ego breaks in two: you begin
to think of yourself in the third person. —*The Seagull*

♦

Rich men were driving to and fro on the road, and every rich
man had a ham and a bottle of vodka in his hands.
—"The Shoemaker and the Devil"

♦

Ah, when you drink you feel nothing, but now. . . ah, I wish
I had never looked at it, the cursed vodka! Truly it is the
blood of Satan! —"Too Early"

♦

Near the books there always stood a decanter of vodka, and a salted
cucumber or a pickled apple lay beside it, not on a plate, but on the
baize table-cloth. Every half-hour he would pour himself out a glass of
vodka and drink it without taking his eyes off the book. —"Ward No. 6"

♦

When we sat down to table he filled my glass with vodka, and,
smiling helplessly, I drank it; he put a piece of ham on my plate
and I ate it submissively. —"The Wife"

165

RANDOM STATS, PART XII: FAST FOOD

98 percent: White Castle hamburger stands resembling white castles.

47 million: Daily number of McDonald's customers worldwide.

30,000-plus: Number of McDonald's restaurants worldwide.

119: Number of countries in which McDonald's has restaurants.

$175,000: Minimum nonborrowed personal resources a person must have to qualify for a McDonald's franchise.

100: Approximate annual number of new McDonald's franchisees.

$40.6 billion: 2001 annual systemwide McDonald's sales.

600: Calories in a Big Mac.

1,016: Total Carl's Jr. restaurants.

59: International Carl's Jr. restaurants.

$14.75: First-day business revenues in 1941 for Carl N. Karcher, founder of Carl's Jr. restaurants.

$1.4 billion: Fiscal year 2004 revenues for CKE Restaurants, Inc., the business founded by Carl N. Karcher.

11,220: Burger King restaurants in 60 countries worldwide.

270 million: Pounds of beef used annually by Burger King restaurants.

2.1 billion: Hamburgers sold annually in Burger King restaurants.

553,170: Pounds of bacon used monthly by Burger King restaurants.

518 million: Pounds of French fries used annually by Burger King.

37 cents: Original price of Burger King's Whopper sandwich in 1957.

6,535: Restaurants in the Wendy's Old Fashioned Hamburgers chain in the United States, Canada, and internationally.

35 million-plus: Customers served weekly in the United States by Taco Bell.

6,500-plus: Taco Bell restaurants in the United States.

280-plus: Taco Bell restaurants operating in Canada, the Caribbean, Latin America, and Europe.

Almost 1,000: Ice cream varieties in the "flavor library" of Baskin-Robbins (31 Flavors).

Almost 3 million: People served across the United States by Baskin-Robbins on "Free Scoop Night," May 3, 2000, when the company donated money for each scoop served to First Book, a nonprofit literacy organization.

4,600-plus: Baskin-Robbins stores in the United States (2,500-plus) and in 52 other countries.

$30 billion: Annual volume of U.S. pizza restaurant industry, according to National Association of Pizza Operators.

61,269: Approximate number of pizzerias in the United States , according to National Association of Pizza Operators.

9 million: Miles covered weekly in the United States by delivery drivers for Domino's Pizza.

1.2 million: Pizzas sold by Domino's on Super Bowl Sunday 2003 (February 1).

46: Average number of pizza slices eaten annually by each person in the United States.

84: Number of countries in which Pizza Hut, the world's largest pizza company, operates.

$600: Initial investment capital two college-age brothers in Kansas borrowed from their mother to start Pizza Hut.

11: Number of herbs and spices in the secret seasoning blend developed by Colonel Harland Sanders for the 1939 launch of his Original Recipe Kentucky Fried Chicken.

1 billion-plus: Kentucky Fried Chicken meals served annually in more than 80 countries.

250,000 miles: Annual distance traveled by Colonel Sanders to visit his restaurants until his death in 1980 at the age of 90.

$105: Social Security check used by Colonel Sanders to finance the franchising of the Kentucky Fried Chicken restaurants.

$2 million: Amount for which Colonel Sanders sold his interest in Kentucky Fried Chicken to an investment group in 1964.

$840 million: Approximate purchase price paid to RJR Nabisco, Inc., by PepsiCo, Inc., in October 1986 for Kentucky Fried Chicken.

380: Calories in one KFC Original Recipe chicken breast.

45 percent: Calories from fat in one KFC Original Recipe breast.

140: Calories in one KFC Original Recipe drumstick.

51.4 percent: Calories from fat in one KFC Original Recipe drumstick.

140: Calories in one KFC Original Recipe breast without skin or breading.

19.28 percent: Calories from fat in one KFC Original Recipe breast without skin or breading.

21,629: Subway restaurants in 76 countries, as of late 2004 (number updated daily on company Web site, www.subway.com).

$5.7 billion: Annual worldwide sales in Subway restaurants.

$12,500: Franchise fee to open a Subway restaurant.

$116,400 to $250,735: Range of estimated costs to open a Subway franchise.

$1 million: Personal/business net worth (with liquidity of $500,000) required to become an Arby's franchisee.

THE LAST DINNER FOR FIRST-CLASS PASSENGERS ON THE RMS TITANIC, APRIL 14, 1912

First Course
Hors d'Oeuvres
Oysters
◆

Second Course
Consommé Olga[1]
Cream of Barley
◆

Third Course
Poached Salmon with Mousseline Sauce, Cucumbers
◆

Fourth Course
Filet Mignons Lili[2]
Sauté of Chicken, Lyonnaise[3]
Vegetable Marrow Farci
◆

Fifth Course
Lamb, Mint Sauce
Roast Duckling, Apple Sauce
Sirloin of Beef, Chateau Potatoes[4]
Green Peas
Creamed Carrots
Boiled Rice
Parmentier[5] and Boiled New Potatoes
◆

Sixth Course
Punch Romaine[6]
◆

Seventh Course
Roast Squab and Cress
◆

Eighth Course
Cold Asparagus Vinaigrette
◆

Ninth Course
Pate de Foie Gras
Celery
◆

Tenth Course
Waldorf Pudding[7]
Peaches in Chartreuse Jelly
Chocolate and Vanilla Éclairs
French Ice Cream

1. Clear broth garnished with bone marrow.
2. Garnished with foie gras, artichoke hearts, and black truffles.
3. Most likely with sautéed onions, garlic, and a tomato-enriched wine-and-cognac sauce.
4. Olive-shaped pieces of potato roasted in butter and garnished with parsley.
5. Small cubes of potato roasted in butter and garnished with parsley.
6. A blend of Champagne; wine, orange and lemon juices; and syrup over crushed ice.
7. Vanilla pudding with nutmeg, apples, and raisins.

TEA AND PERFECT HAPPINESS

When they had run and danced themselves dry, the girls quickly dressed and sat down to the fragrant tea. They sat on the northern side of the grove, in the yellow sunshine facing the slope of the grassy hill, alone in a little wild world of their own. The tea was hot and aromatic, there were delicious little sandwiches of cucumber and of caviare, and winy cakes.

'Are you happy, Prune?' cried Ursula in delight, looking at her sister.

'Ursula, I'm perfectly happy,' replied Gudrun gravely, looking at the westering sun.

'So am I.'

When they were together, doing the things they enjoyed, the two sisters were quite complete in a perfect world of their own. And this was one of the perfect moments of freedom and delight, such as children alone know, when all seems a perfect and blissful adventure.

When they had finished tea, the two girls sat on, silent and serene.

—*Women in Love* (1920), D. H. Lawrence

BREAKFAST ON THE MISSISSIPPI

They came back to camp wonderfully refreshed, glad-hearted, and ravenous; and they soon had the camp-fire blazing up again. Huck found a spring of clear cold water close by, and the boys made cups of broad oak or hickory leaves, and felt that water, sweetened with such a wildwood charm as that, would be a good enough substitute for coffee. While Joe was slicing bacon for breakfast, Tom and Huck asked him to hold on a minute; they stepped to a promising nook in the river-bank and threw in their lines; almost immediately they had reward. Joe had not had time to get impatient before they were back again with some handsome bass, a couple of sun-perch and a small catfish—provisions enough for quite a family. They fried the fish with the bacon, and were astonished; for no fish had ever seemed so delicious before. They did not know that the quicker a fresh-water fish is on the fire after he is caught the better he is; and they reflected little upon what a sauce open-air sleeping, open-air exercise, bathing, and a large ingredient of hunger make, too.

—*The Adventures of Tom Sawyer* (1881), Mark Twain

EATING AND DRINKING ACROSS THE MAP, PART X:
SEASONINGS AND CONDIMENTS DEPARTMENT

Anise, Pennsylvania
Basil, Kansas
Caraway, Arkansas
Cayenne, Massachusetts
Cinnamon Acres, Arkansas
Clove, New York
Dill, Alabama (also Tennessee)
Ginger, Texas (also Washington)
Ginger Hill, Illinois
Ketchuptown, South Carolina
Mace, Idaho (also Indiana, New Mexico, and West Virginia)
Mint, Arizona (also Tennessee)
Mustard, Pennsylvania

Nutmeg Creek, California
Parsley, West Virginia
Pepper, Delaware (also Virginia and West Virginia)
Rosemary, Alabama (also California, Maine, Mississippi, and North Carolina)
Saffron Walden, England
Sage, Arkansas (also California, Nevada, and Wyoming)
Salt, England
Salt Creek, South Australia
Salt Flat, Texas
Salt Fork, Oklahoma

Salt Gap, Texas
Salt Hill, Ireland
Salt Lake, South Australia
Salt Lake City, Utah
Salt Lick, Kentucky

Salt Point, New York
Salt Springs, Florida
Salt Wells, Nevada
Vanilla, Pennsylvania

SOME NATIONAL FOOD OBSERVANCES: DECEMBER

1st:	National Pie Day
2nd:	National Fritters Day
3rd:	National Ice Cream Box Day
4th:	National Cookie Day
5th:	National Sachertorte Day
6th:	National Gazpacho Day
7th:	National Cotton Candy Day
8th:	National Brownie Day
9th:	National Pastry Day
11th:	National Noodle Ring Day
12th:	National Ambrosia Day
13th:	National Cocoa Day
14th:	National Bouillabaisse Day
15th:	National Lemon Cupcake Day
16th:	National Chocolate-Covered Anything Day
17th:	National Maple Syrup Day
18th:	National Roast Suckling Pig Day
19th:	National Oatmeal Muffin Day
21st:	National French Fried Shrimp Day
	National Hamburger Day
22nd:	National Date-Nut Bread Day
23rd:	National Pfeffernüsse Day
24th:	National Eggnog Day
25th:	National Pumpkin Pie Day
26th:	National Candy Cane Day
27th:	National Fruitcake Day
28th:	National Chocolate Day (also 29th)
29th:	National Chocolate Day (also 28th)
30th:	National Bicarbonate of Soda Day
31st:	National Champagne Day

SOBERING WORDS ON WINE AND BREAD

3:9–10 Honour the LORD with thy substance, and with the first fruits of all thine increase: So shall thy barns be filled with plenty, and thy presses shall burst out with new wine.

4:17 For they eat the bread of wickedness, and drink the wine of violence.

6:26 For by means of a whorish woman a man is brought to a piece of bread: and the adultress will hunt for the precious life.

9:1–2 Wisdom hath builded her house, she hath hewn out her seven pillars: She hath killed her beasts; she hath mingled her wine; she hath also furnished her table.

9:5 Come, eat of my bread, and drink of the wine which I have mingled.

9:17 Stolen waters are sweet, and bread eaten in secret is pleasant.

12:9 He that is despised, and that a servant, is better than he that honoureth himself, and lacketh bread.

12:11 He that tilleth his land shall be satisfied with bread: but he that followeth vain persons is void of understanding.

20:1 Wine is a mocker, strong drink is raging: and whosoever is deceived thereby is not wise.

20:13 Love not sleep, lest thou come to poverty; open thine eyes, and thou shalt be satisfied with bread.

20:17 Bread of deceit is sweet to a man; but afterwards his mouth shall be filled with gravel.

21:17 He that loveth pleasure shall be a poor man: he that loveth wine and oil shall not be rich.

22:9 He that hath a bountiful eye shall be blessed; for he giveth of his bread to the poor.

23:6–7 Eat thou not the bread of him that hath an evil eye, neither desire thou his dainty meats: For as he thinketh in his heart, so is he: Eat and drink, saith he to thee; but his heart is not with thee.

23:20 Be not among winebibbers; among riotous eaters of flesh: For the drunkard and the glutton shall come to poverty: and drowsiness shall clothe a man with rags.

23:29–31 Who hath woe? who hath sorrow? who hath contentions? who hath babbling? who hath wounds without cause? who hath redness of eye? They that tarry long at the wine; they that go to seek mixed wine. Look not thou upon the wine when it is red, when it giveth his colour in the cup, when it moveth itself aright.

25:21 If thine enemy be hungry, give him bread to eat; and if he be thirsty, give him water to drink.

28:19 He that tilleth his land shall have plenty of bread: but he that followeth after vain persons shall have poverty enough.

28:21 To have respect of persons is not good: for, for a piece of bread that man will transgress.

31:4–5 It is not for kings, O Lemuel, it is not for kings to drink wine; nor for princes strong drink: Lest they drink, and forget the law, and pervert the judgment of any of the afflicted.

31:6 Give strong drink unto him that is ready to perish, and wine unto those that be of heavy hearts.

31:21 She looketh well to the ways of her household, and eateth not the bread of idleness.

—Proverbs (King James Version)

FUN WITH FOOD & DRINK, PART VI:
READING TURKISH COFFEE GROUNDS

Throughout the Middle East, the thick, sweet coffee commonly known as Turkish coffee leaves a sludgy residue of grounds on the bottom of the small cup in which it is served. Traditionally, these grounds may be read in an informal fortune-telling session.

1. **Brew the coffee.** For each cup, start with one tablespoon of very finely ground Mocha coffee, three ounces of cold water, and one teaspoon of sugar (more or less, depending on desired sweetness). Put them in an ibrik, a traditional Turkish coffee pot made of brass, with a long handle and narrower top than bottom. Cook over medium-low heat until the liquid boils and froths up. Remove from the heat and stir until the froth settles. Heat, froth, remove from heat, and stir again. Repeat once more, pouring the coffee into demitasses while still frothing, shaking the pot while pouring to ensure some froth pours into each cup.
2. **Drink the coffee.** Encourage guests to sip and savor the coffee slowly, draining their cups until they reach the very thick grounds at the bottom.
3. **Invert the cups.** Demonstrating for your guests, quickly invert your cup into its saucer with a turn of your wrist, taking special care while doing so not to fling the grounds at anyone. Encourage your guests to turn their cups over in the same way. Leave the inverted cups for about five minutes to allow the grounds to drip down the insides and dry slightly.
4. **Read the fortunes.** One by one, ask each guest to turn his or her cup back right side up. As a group, study the patterns made by the grounds inside each person's cup, interpreting them with imagination to predict a fortune. Some examples: wavelike ripples predict a journey overseas or a beach vacation; jagged peaks and valley may mean tumultuous emotions; a shapely profile may foretell new romance; and so on. Be creative!

A GOOD ARGUMENT FOR DESSERT

Any dietician will tell you that a running foot of apple strudel contains four times the vitamins of a bushel of beans.

—S. J. Perelman (1904–1979)

SUBSTITUTIONS IN BAKING

For . . .	Substitute . . .
Baking powder, 1 tsp	½ tsp cream of tartar + ⅓ tsp baking soda
Butter or margarine, 1 cup	⅞ cup shortening + pinch of salt
Buttermilk, 1 cup	1 cup milk + 1 Tbsp lemon juice *or* 1 cup milk + ½ Tbsp cream of tartar
Chocolate, semisweet, 1 oz	1 oz unsweetened chocolate + 1 Tbsp sugar *or* 3 Tbsps cocoa powder + 1 Tbsp vegetable oil
Condensed milk, 1 cup	⅓ cup evaporated milk + ¾ cup sugar + 2 Tbsps butter, heated, stirring, until dissolved
Flour, all-purpose, 1 cup	1 cup + 2 Tbsps cake flour *or* ¾ cup bran flour + ¼ cup all-purpose flour *or* ⅞ cup rice flour *or* 1¼ cups rye flour
Flour, self-rising, 1 cup	1 cup all-purpose flour + 1 tsp baking powder + ½ tsp salt *or* flour, cake, sifted, 1 cup
Milk, 1 cup	1 cup water + 2 Tbsps butter *or* 1 cup concentrated fruit juice
Sour cream, 1 cup	1 cup buttermilk or yogurt + 1 Tbsp cornstarch
Sugar, granulated, 1 cup	1 cup corn syrup* *or* brown sugar, 1 cup *or* ⅞ cup honey* *or* ½ cup maple syrup + ¼ cup corn syrup* *or* 1 cup confectioner's sugar + 1 Tbsp cornstarch

* With liquid sweeteners, reduce other liquids in the recipe by about ¼ cup.

SOME MILESTONES IN FOOD AND DRINK HISTORY:
20TH CENTURY AD

1902: Renowned French chef August Escoffier publishes his cookbook *Le Guide Culinaire.*

1902: National Biscuit Co. launches its animal crackers.

1907: Hershey launches its milk chocolate Kisses.

1908: Frenchman Phillippe Matthieu opens Phillippe's near downtown Los Angeles, where he invents the broth-soaked French dip in 1918.

1909: Melitta Bentz, a German housewife, and her busband Hugo introduce the Melitta drip coffee filter.

1914: African American scientist George Washington Carver shares his extensive experimental findings on the many uses for the peanut.

1915: Chicago's J. L. Kraft & Bros. introduces a processed mild Cheddar process that comes to be dubbed American cheese.

1920: In January, the 18th Amendment to the U.S. Constitution prohibits the transportation, importation, exportation, or sale of alcohol.

1924: Italian-born chef Caesar Cardini invents the Caesar salad at his restaurant in Tijuana, Mexico, just across the border from California.

1930: Birds Eye brand frozen vegetables are launched in Massachusetts, using freezing techniques developed by inventor Clarence Birdseye.

1930: Continental Baking launches a cream-filled sponge cake, the Hostess Twinkie.

1931: General Mills launches Bisquick baking mix.

1932: In San Antonio, Texas, the Doolin family launches Frito corn chips.

1933: At the Toll House Inn in Whitman, Massachusetts, Ruth Wakefield develops the Toll House chocolate chip cookie.

1933: Prohibition is repealed in the United States.

1936: American bandleader Fred Waring launches the first commercial electric kitchen blender.

1936: Orangina sparkling orange drink launches in Algeria and France.

1937: Britain's Rowntree and Co. renames its recently introduced Chocolate Crisp bar the Kit Kat.

1937: The first shopping cart is introduced in Oklahoma City.

1937: The George A. Hormel Co. introduces SPAM, short for "spiced ham."

1938: *Larousse Gastronomique* is first published in Paris.

1939: Cardboard cartons first begin to replace glass bottles for milk in the United States.

1940: Richard and Maurice McDonald open their first drive-in hamburger stands in Southern California.

1941: General Mills introduces Cheerios.

1945: Chemist Earl W. Tupper launches a company to market his sealable airtight plastic food containers, Tupperware.

1947: In Waltham, Massachusetts, Raytheon introduces the Radarange, the first microwave oven.

1948: In Southern California, brothers-in-law Burton Baskin and Irvine Robbins found Baskin-Robbins, known as the home of "31 Flavors."

1954: Chuck Williams opens his first cookware store in Sonoma, California. Four years later, Williams-Sonoma will open in San Francisco, soon to benefit from a booming interest in gourmet cooking in the United States.

1955: Harlan Sanders launches his Kentucky Fried Chicken franchises.

1961: Julia Child and her Parisian cooking school partners Simone Beck and Louisette Bertholle publish *Mastering the Art of French Cooking.*

1972: Alice Waters opens Chez Panisse in Berkeley, pioneering California cuisine.

1973: Inventor and entrepreneur Carl Sontheimer introduces the Cuisinart food processor to America.

1978: Ben Cohen and Jerry Greenfield launch their first ice cream shop, Ben & Jerry's, in Burlington, Vermont.

1981: Actor Paul Newman launches his Newman's Own brand of high-quality packaged food products, from which all profits are donated to charity.

1987: In Seattle, Washington, Howard Schultz launches Starbucks coffee.

1993: Launch of The Food Network on cable television in the United States.

IN OTHER WORDS, WINE

O, for a draught of vintage! that hath been
Cool'd a long age in the deep-delved earth,
Tasting of Flora and the country green,
Dance, and Provençal song, and sunburnt mirth!
O for a beaker full of the warm South,
Full of the true, the blushful Hippocrene,
With beaded bubbles winking at the brim,
And purple-stained mouth;
That I might drink, and leave the world unseen,
And with thee fade away into the forest dim.
—"Ode to a Nightingale" (1819), John Keats

SOME FOOD AND DRINK WEB SITES—IN THEIR OWN WORDS

The following list focuses on select Web sites, some of which served as reference sources for this book that provide a wealth of useful and interesting information related to food and drink. Please note that some of them are also commercial enterprises that aim to sell you products.

AsiaCuisine.com *Slogan:* "Asia's leading food and beverage portal."

BBC.co.uk/food The extensive food pages of the British Broadcasting Corporation's Web site. Sections include TV and Radio, Back to Basics, Chefs, Recipes, News and Events, In Season, and Contact Us.

DineSite.com *Slogan:* "World-class Guides to Local Dining." *Description:* "Brings you world-class dining guides for over 12,000 towns—descriptions, photos, menus and more!"

ecookbooks.com *Proper name:* Jessica's Biscuit. *Slogan:* "America's Cookbook Store™." *Description:* "The approach is simple: offer the world's most comprehensive collection of cookbooks with unparalleled service at the lowest prices." Includes Chef's Corner and a growing recipes database.

Epicurious.com *Slogan:* "The world's greatest recipe collection." From the publisher of *Bon Appétit* and *Gourmet* magazines, sections include Recipes, Features, Cooking, Drinking, Restaurants, and Shop.

FoodandWine.com From the magazine of the same name. Includes extensive information on wines, cooking, entertaining, and travel, along with shopping opportunities.

FoodLines.com *Description:* "FoodLines is dedicated to providing reliable food and nutrition information on the Internet." Sections include Latest News, Food Smart Nutrition Analysis, Recipe Swap, Healthy Eating, Marketplace, and Tools.

FoodReference.com *Description:* "Both a reference and casual browsing site . . . long articles on food history and usage; short food facts and trivia; an extensive collection of quotes; who's who in food; cooking tips; culinary humor, poems and crossword puzzles, and a Culinary Calendar. Recipes, modern, classic and historical are also presented."

FoodSubs.com *Proper name:* The Cook's Thesaurus. *Description:* "A cooking encyclopedia that covers thousands of ingredients and kitchen tools. Entries include pictures, descriptions, synonyms, pronunciations, and suggested substitutions."

FoodNetwork.com Web site of cable television's Food Network. Sections include Cooking, Recipes, TV, Entertaining, Wine & Drinks, Contests & Offers, and Store, along with chat rooms and feature articles.

GlobalGourmet.com *Description:* "The first food and cooking 'magazine' on the World Wide Web." Includes multiple informative departments, features, recipe archives, tips, contests, and shopping.

Gourmetspot.com *Slogan:* "Simplifying the Search for the Best Culinary Content Online." *Description:* "Designed to break through the information overload of the Web to bring the best food and beverage sites together with insightful editorials in one convenient, user-friendly spot. Sites featured on GourmetSpot.com are hand-selected by our editorial team for their exceptional quality, content and utility—and of course their good taste."

iDrink.com *Description:* "The web's favourite destination for drink information is being transformed from just a drink and recipe database to the fun, exciting, interactive, refreshing new world of mixing, drinking, shopping and sipping. Enter to enjoy the complete online drink experience!"

OutofTheFryingPan.com *Slogan:* "Food, fun & flavor from your queens of cuisine." Sections include Chef Tips, Cocktail ABCs, Cooking with the Rock Stars, Cookbook Guide, Entertaining, Food Festivals, Fresh Off the Grill, Gadgets a-Go-Go, Greg's Top Five Lists, Herb & Spice Encyclopedia, Just Desserts, Kitchen Math, Master Recipe Index, Merchandise, Message Boards, Presentation 101, Speed Queen (quick dishes), and Writer Profiles.

SauteWednesday.com Extensive, highly literate site including content from and links to other food Web sites, newspaper food sections and food magazines, video and radio, restaurant dining guides, wine information, blogs, and more.

Wine.com *Description:* "Shop the largest online assortment of wines from around the world." Includes extensive, highly informative section on wine.

THE FATHER OF CHAMPAGNE SPEAKS

Brothers, come quickly. I am tasting stars!
—Dom Pierre Pérignon (1638–1716)

SOME FOOD REFERENCE BOOKS—IN THEIR OWN WORDS

A wealth of books have been published that provide fascinating, detailed information on food. Here are some favorites, several of which served as reference sources for this book.

Corriher, Shirley O. *CookWise: The Hows and Whys of Successful Cooking.* New York: William Morrow, 1997. "There are over 230 outstanding recipes . . . but here each recipe serves not only to please the palate but to demonstrate the roles of ingredients and techniques."

Davidson, Alan. *The Oxford Companion to Food.* London: Oxford University Press, 1999. "Twenty years in the making, here is the long-awaited magnum opus from one of the world's great authorities on the history and use of food . . . packed with 2,650 delightfully written A-Z entries."

Green, Jonathon, editor. *Consuming Passions.* New York: Fawcett Columbine, 1985. "A feast of quotations celebrating food and the art of dining."

Herbst, Sharon Tyler. *Never Eat More Than You Can Lift and Other Food Quotes and Quips: 1,500 Notable Quotables About Edibles and Potables.* New York: Broadway Books, 1997. "An 'appeteasing' collection of racy, wicked, funny, informative, and historical quotations about food and drink."

Herbst, Sharon Tyler. *The New Food Lover's Companion: Comprehensive Definitions of Over 3000 Food, Wine, and Culinary Terms.* Hauppauge, New York: Barron's Educational, 1995. "For anybody who cooks—or who simply loves food—here's a terrific reference source and an outstanding cookbook supplement."

Kiple, Kenneth F. and Kriemheld Coneè Ornelas, Editors. *The Cambridge World History of Food.* London: Cambridge University Press, 2000. "An undertaking without parallel or precedent, this monumental two-volume work encapsulates much of what is known of the history of food and nutrition throughout the span of human life on earth."

Kolpas, Norman. *The Gourmet's Lexicon.* New York: Perigee, 1983. "Presents a lively guide to the basic terms every epicure must know."

Lang, George. *Lang's Compendium of Culinary Nonsense and Trivia.* New York: Clarkson N. Potter, Inc., 1980. "An amusing, helpful, vital, trivial, surprising, shocking, revealing, I-knew-it-all collection of facts, fancies, and fantasies."

Labensky, Steven, Gaye G. Ingram, and Sarah R. Labensky. *Webster's New World Dictionary of Culinary Arts*. New York: Prentice Hall, 2000. "The most authoritative, complete glossary of the culinary arts: now includes over 25,000 entries!"

Lang, Jennifer Harvey, editor. *Larousse Gastronomique: The New American Edition of the World's Greatest Culinary Encyclopedia*. New York: Crown Publishers, 1988. "It is truly an encyclopedia—from Abaisse (a sheet of uncooked pastry) to Zwieback (a cracker)—that explains virtually everything there is to know about classical cuisine."

McGee, Harold. *On Food and Cooking*. New York: Scribner, 1984. "A unique blend of culinary lore and scientific explanation that examines food—its history, its make-up, and its behavior when we cook it, cool it, dice it, age it, or otherwise prepare it for eating."

Robbins, Maria Polushkin, editor. *A Cook's Alphabet of Quotations*. Hopewell, New Jersey: The Ecco Press, 1991. "A motley group of wits and other opinionated personalities . . . all reveal their honest thoughts on one of life's most elementary pleasures."

Robbins, Maria Polushkin, editor. *The Cook's Quotation Book: A Literary Feast*. New York: Penguin Books, 1984. "This book is the felicitous result of the two great and guilty pleasures of my life—eating and reading."

Stobart, Tom. *The Cook's Encyclopedia: Ingredients & Processes*. London: B. T. Batsford, Ltd., 1980. "Its comprehensive coverage . . . gathers together a vast amount of valuable information that is available in fragments scattered through a large range of works on cooking and food science."

Tannahill, Reay. *Food in History*. New York: Three Rivers Press, 1995. "An enthralling world history of food from prehistoric times to the present."

Trager, James. *The Food Chronology: A Food Lover's Compendium of Events and Anecdotes, from Prehistory to the Present*. New York: Henry Holt, 1995. "A sweeping history of food that is both a thorough reference and a delight to read."

Wasserman, Pauline, with Sheldon Wasserman. *Don't Ask Your Waiter*. New York: Stein and Day, 1978. "A guide to understanding the menus in fine continental restaurants."

Williams, Chuck, general editor. *Williams-Sonoma Kitchen Companion: The A to Z Guide to Everyday Cooking, Equipment & Ingredients*. Alexandria, Virginia: Time-Life Books, 2000. "An all-purpose, easy-to-use guide for the home cook. Whether you're curious about a common cooking instruction or need to find a quick substitution for an ingredient, *Kitchen Companion* comes to the rescue."

SOME DRINK REFERENCE BOOKS—IN THEIR OWN WORDS

A wealth of books have been published that provide fascinating, detailed information on drink. Here are some favorites, several of which served as reference sources for this book.

Foley, Ray. *Bartending for Dummies.* New York: For Dummies, 2003. "Everything you need to shake, stir, and serve like a pro."

Herbst, Sharon Tyler, and Ron Herbst. *The Ultimate A-to-Z Bar Guide.* New York: Broadway Books, 1998. "A one-stop, user-friendly cocktail guide featuring more than 1,000 drink recipes and 600 definitions for cocktail-related terms."

Immer, Andrea. *Great Wine Made Simple: Straight Talk from a Master Sommelier.* New York: Broadway Books, 2000. "Never again will you have to fear pricey bottles that don't deliver, snobby wine waiters, foreign terminology, or encyclopedic restaurant wine lists."

McCarthy, Mary Ewing-Mulligan, and Piero Antinori. *Wine for Dummies.* New York: For Dummies, 2003. "The authors deliver just what ordinary mortals need to navigate the wine list at a restaurant or the wine aisle at a store, select a great bottle, and truly enjoy it."

Williams-Sonoma. *The Bar Guide.* Des Moines, Iowa: Oxmoor House, 2002. "All you need to know about the art of mixing cocktails and other drinks."

Williams-Sonoma. *The Wine Guide.* Des Moines, Iowa: Oxmoor House, 2002. "All you need to know to choose and enjoy wine."

SOME OTHER FOOD BOOKS BY NORMAN KOLPAS

The Bel-Air Book of Southern California Food and Entertaining. New York: Crown, 1991.

The Big Little Peanut Butter Cookbook. Chicago: Contemporary Books, 1990.

Breakfast and Brunch Book. Los Angeles: H.P. Books, 1988.

Britain. New York: Running Press, 1990.

Buongiorno! Breakfast & Brunch Italian Style. Chicago: Contemporary Books, 2001.

The Chili Cookbook. Los Angeles: H.P. Books, 1991.

The Chocolate Lover's Companion. New York: Quick Fox/Putnam, 1978.

The Coffee Lover's Companion. New York: Quick Fox/Putnam, 1978, and London: John Murray, 1979.

Comforting Foods. New York: Macmillan, 1999.
A Cup of Coffee. New York: Grove Press, 1993.
Gourmet Sandwiches. Los Angeles: H.P. Books, 1993.
The Gourmet's Lexicon. New York: Perigee, 1983.
Hors d'Oeuvres. Los Angeles: H.P. Books, 1990.
Main Dish Salads. Pleasantville, New York: Reader's Digest Books, 1998.
Michael's Cookbook (coauthored with Michael McCarty). New York: Macmillan, 1989.
Modern Southwest Cuisine (coauthored with John Rivera Sedlar). New York: Simon & Schuster, 1986, and Berkeley, California: Ten Speed Press, 1994.
More Pasta Light. Chicago: Contemporary Books, 1995.
More Pasta Presto. Chicago: Contemporary Books, 1997.
Pasta Gusto. Chicago: Contemporary Books, 1994.
Pasta Light. Chicago: Contemporary Books, 1990.
Pasta Menus. Chicago: Contemporary Books, 1993.
Pasta Presto. Chicago: Contemporary Books, 1988.
Pizza California Style. Chicago: Contemporary Books, 1989.
Pizza Presto. Chicago: Contemporary Books, 1996.
The Quick Grill Artist. New York: Clarkson N. Potter Publishers, 2002.
Southwest the Beautiful Cookbook. New York: Collins, 1994.
The Southwestern Companion. New York: BDD, 1991.
Sweet Indulgences. Los Angeles: H.P. Books, 1990.
Whole Meal Salads. Chicago: Contemporary Books, 1992.
Williams-Sonoma Kitchen Library: Breakfasts & Brunches. Alexandria, Virginia: Time-Life Books, 1997.
Williams-Sonoma Kitchen Library: Soups. Alexandria, Virginia: Time-Life Books, 1993.
The World's Best Noodles. Chicago: Contemporary Books, 1993.

FOR THE PLEASURE OF SAVOURING

Correcting copy was frustrating. Often I slashed through words, sentences, paragraphs, scribbling "Get rid of Time-Lifese," "Stop being cute," "Keep it simple" and so forth. Unfortunately, the writers loved reading my comments, in particular one, Norman Kolpas, who wrote more and more outrageously for the pleasure of savouring my reactions.

—*Reflexions* (1999), Richard Olney

FAMOUS LAST WORDS ON FOOD AND DRINK

Herewith, reported dying words uttered by famous lovers of food and drink from varied walks of life.

Tallulah Bankhead (1902–1968), American actress:
". . . codeine . . . bourbon . . ."

◆

Humphrey Bogart (1899–1957), American actor:
"I should never have switched from Scotch to Martinis."

◆

Johannes Brahams (1833–1897), German composer:
"Ah, that tastes nice. Thank you."

◆

**Pierette Brillat-Savarin, aunt of Jean-Anthelme Brillat-Savarin
(1755–1826), author of *The Physiology of Taste:***
"I feel the end approaching. Quick, bring me my
dessert, coffee, and liqueur."

◆

Marie-Antoine Carême (1784–1833), renowned French chef and author:
"My lad, the quenelles de sole were splendid, but the peas were poor.
You should shake the pan gently, all the time, like this."

◆

Christopher "Kit" Carson (1809–1868), American frontiersman:
"Wish I had time for just one more bowl of chili."

◆

Anton Chekhov (1860–1904), Russian author/playwright:
"It's been a long time since I've drunk Champagne."

◆

Paul Claudel (1868–1955), French poet and diplomat:
"Doctor, do you think it could have been the sausage?"

◆

**Lou Costello (1906–1959), American vaudeville star
and film/TV comedian:**
"That was the best ice-cream soda I ever tasted."

◆

Millard Fillmore (1800–1874), American president:
"The nourishment is palatable."

◆

John Maynard Keynes (1883–1946), British economist:
"I wish I'd drunk more Champagne."

◆

Pablo Picasso (1881–1973), Spanish painter:
"Drink to me!"

◆

William Pitt (1759–1806), British prime minister:
"I think I could eat one of Bellamy's veal pies."

◆

Robert the Bruce (1274–1329), Scottish king:
"Now, God be with you, my dear children. I have breakfasted
with you and shall sup with my Lord Jesus Christ."

◆

Dylan Thomas (1914–1953), Welsh poet:
"I've had eighteen straight whiskies. I do believe that is a record."

INDEX

The Adventures of Tom Sawyer (Twain), 170
African, North, food, 46
Africans, forbidden foods, 59
Alcohol, geographic place names, 56–57
Alcott, Louisa May, 34
Aldrich's Beef & Ice Cream Parlor, 116
Alexander II, Tsar, 96
Alexander III, Tsar, 96
The Alice B. Toklas Cookbook (Toklas), 135
Alice's Adventures in Wonderland (Carroll), 53
All's Well That Ends Well (Shakespeare), 102
Anagrams, prophetic food personality
  name, 142
Antony and Cleopatra (Shakespeare), 103
Apples, Johnny Appleseed and, 162
Arby's franchise, costs to open, 167
The Art of Cookery (Glasse), 155
Austen, Jane, 117
Avocado, Haas, 126

Babette's Feast (movie), 71
Baby Ruth candy, 130
Baked Alaska dessert, 162
Bakery and pastry, geographic place
  names, 99
Baking, substitutions, 175
Balzac, Honore de, 76, 87
Banana, slicing without peeling, 48
Bankhead, Tallulah, 184
Barbecue Industry Association, 129
Baskin-Robbins ice cream stores
  founding of, 177
  statistics, 166
Beard, James, 37, 142
Beatles, The, 114
Béchamel sauce, 130, 134
Beecher, Henry Ward, 109
Beef
  steaks, 116–117
  Stroganoff, 131
  Wellington, 131
Beer
  Coors, 163
  Guinness, 155
  Heineken, 104
  Lowenbrau, 75
  phrases related to, 97
  purity law, 104
  statistics, 143
Bellini cocktail, 130
The Bell Jar (Plath), 31

Ben & Jerry's ice cream stores, 177
Beverages
  geographic place names, 135
  hot, statistics, 139
  soft drinks, statistics, 36
Bhagavad Gita, food prayers from, 41
Bible, dietary laws from, 26–27
Bierce, Ambrose, *Devil's Dictionary*, 136
Big Night (movie), 72
Birds Eye frozen foods, 176
Blessings, *see* Prayers
Bogart, Humphrey, 184
Boston Cooking School Cookbook (Farmer), 163
Boston Tea Party, 21, 155
Boswell, James, 29, 59, 121
Bottled water, statistics, 21
Brahams, Johannes, 184
Brandy, 121
Bread
  biblical proverbs about, 172–173
  storage time, 153
  unleavened, origins of, 146
Brewery, *see* Beer
Brillat-Savarin, Jean-Anthelme, 162, 184
Brillat-Savarin, Pierette, 184
British Isles, food, 86–87
Burger King restaurants, statistics, 166
Burns, Robert, 106, 155
Burnt Food, Museum of, 141
The Butcher's Wife (movie), 71
Byron, Lord, 32

Cadbury chocolate, 162
Caesar, Julius, 17
Caesar salad, 176
Campbell soup company, 163
Candy
  Baby Ruth, 130
  Candy Wrapper Museum, 140
  Jelly Belly, 32
  Kit Kat, 176
  PEZ, 126–127
  syrup stages, 120
  see also Chocolate
Candy Wrapper Museum, 140
Capote, Truman, 160
Caramel, stages of, 120
Carème, Marie-Antoine, 184
Caribbean food, 54–55
Carl's Jr. restaurants, statistics, 166
Carpaccio appetizer, 130

Carroll, Lewis, 53, 123
Carson, Christopher "Kit," 184
Carver, George Washington, 176
"The Cask of Amontillado" (Poe), 115
Catherine II, Czarina, 131
Caviar
  account of, 31
  statistics, 29
  terms related to, 134
Celsius scale, 118
Cereal
  Kellogg's, 163
  Lucky Charms, 142
Champagne, 155
  bottle sizes, 131
  Dom Pérignon, 134, 179
Charles II, King, 134
Cheese, American, 176
Chekhov, Anton, 184
  on vodka, 164–165
Chemical compounds, 88
Child, Julia, 177
Chili, Cincinnati, options, 69
Chinese
  food, 37
    dim sum, 14
    wine pairing and, 34
  fortune cookies, 138–139
Chocolat (movie), 73
Chocolate
  Aztecs and, 104
  Cadbury, 162
  cocoa powder, 162
  as comfort food, 120
  Hershey, 163, 176
  substitutions for, 175
A Christmas Carol (Dickens), 22, 124
"A Christmas Memory" (Capote), 160
Cincinnati chili, options, 69
On Civility in Children (Erasmus), 16
Claudel, Paul, 185
Cleveland, Grover, 130
Coca-Cola, 36
Cockney rhyming slang, 42–45
Coffee
  Brazilian, 155
  composing a "coffee shot," 147–149
  discovery in Ethiopia, 47
  grounds, reading Turkish, 174
  as literary inspiration, 76
  Melitta drip filter for, 176
  slang words for, 93
  Starbucks, 177
  statistics, 139

"such a cup," 109
Turkish, 53
unsuccessful attempt to place ban on, 104
Vienna coffeehouse, 134
Columbus, Christopher, 75
The Comedy of Errors (Shakespeare), 100
Comfort foods, statistics, 120
The Compleat Angler, Part II (Cotton), 61
Confucius, proverbs of, 56
Consuming Passions: The Anthropology of Eating
  (Farb & Armelagos), 21
Coors Brewery, 163
Cortes, Hernando, 104
Costello, Lou, 185
Cotton, Charles, 61
Crackerjack popcorn snack, 163
Cranford (Gaskell), 144
Cucumber, fate fit for, 29
Cuisinart food processor, 177
Cuisines
  British Isles, 86–87
  Chinese, 14
  Far Eastern, pairing Western wine with, 34
  French, 156–157
  German, Eastern European, and Russian,
    125
  Greek, Turkish, Middle Eastern, and
    North African, 46
  Indian, 140
  Italian, 98–99
  Japanese, 33
  Jewish, 121
  Mexican, Latin American, and
    Caribbean, 54–55
  Pan-Asian, 108–109
  Scandinavian, 159
  Spanish and Portuguese, 129
Culinary Institute of America, 177
Curtiss Candy Company, 130

Dairy, geographic place names, 124
David Copperfield (Dickens), 23
David, Elizabeth, 49
de Gama, Vasco, 75
de' Medici, Caterina, 104
De Re Coquinaria (Apicius), 47
de Richelieu, duc, 155
de Saint-Amant, Marc Antoine, 19
Deuteronomy (Bible), dietary laws of, 26–27
The Devil's Dictionary (Bierce), 136
Dickens, Charles, 22, 111, 124
Dim Sum: Little Bit of Heart (movie), 72
Dim Sum, varieties, 14
Diner, American, slang used in, 92–94

Diner (movie), 70
Dinner Rush (movie), 73
Doctor Marigold (Dickens), 23
Domino's Pizza, statistics, 167
Doneness
  gauging, 61
  temperatures, 79
Don Juan (Gordon & Byron), 32
Dying words, on food and drink, 184–185

Eastern European food, 125
Eat Drink Man Woman (movie), 72
Egg
  forcing into a milk bottle, 89
  storage time, 150
Emma (Austen), 117
Emperors, dinner menu of, 96–97
Endicott, John, 134
Epicurus (Greek philosopher), 17
Erasmus, Desiderius, 16
Escoffier, August, 176
Eskimos, forbidden foods, 59
Essays of Elia (Lamb), 68–69
Ethiopian Christians, forbidden foods, 59
Eyes and Ears (Beecher), 109

Fahrenheit scale, 118, 155
Farb, Peter, 21
Farmer, Fannie, 163
Fear Factor (television show), gross foods
  eaten on, 154
Figures of speech, 62, 63
Fillmore, Millard, 185
FitzGerald, Edward, 14
Flaubert, Gustave, 85
Flowers, edible, 74
Foie gras, statistics, 29
Food
  comfort, statistics, 120
  fast, statistics, 166–167
  fearful, 154
  as figures of speech, 62, 63
  forbidden, 59
  frozen, statistics, 60
  gourmet, statistics, 29
  named after famous people, 130–131
  storage times, 150–153
  Web sites, 178–179
Food Network, 177
Forbidden foods, 59
Forrest Gump (movie), 63
Fortune cookies, fortunes in, 138–139
*The Four Wondrous Properties and Effects of
  Wine* (Merckel), 146

Franklin, Benjamin
  on food and drink, 40–41
  on wine-making, 158–159
French food, 156–157
Fried Green Tomatoes (movie), 71
Fritos corn chips, 176
Frozen food, statistics, 60
Fruit
  storage times of, 152
  varieties of, 14

Gargantua (fictional character), 87
German food, 125
German Purity Law, 113
Gilbert, W. S., 47
God of Cookery (movie), 72
Gordon, George, 32
Gourmet foods, statistics, 29
Grace
  Christian prayers of, 38
  see also Prayers
Grahame, Kenneth, 12
La Grande Bouffe (movie), 70
Great Depression, 21
Great Expectations (Dickens), 23
Greek food, 46
Grey Poupon mustard, 155
Grilling and barbecuing, statistics, 129
Le Guide Culinaire (Escoffer), 176
Guide Michelin (restaurant guidebook), 163
Guinness Beer, 155

Haas avocado, 126
Haggis, 86
"Haggis, Address to a" (Burns), 106–107
Hamburgers
  Burger King, 166
  Carl's Jr., 166
  McDonald's, 166
  Wendy's Old-Fashioned, 166
  White Castle, 166
Hanks, Tom, 63
Hearth, Patio & Barbecue Association, 129
Heinz ketchup, 163
Henri II, King, 104
Henri IV, King, 134
Henry IV, Part 1 (Shakespeare), 101
Henry IV, Part 2 (Shakespeare), 101
Henry V (Shakespeare), 101
Herbert, A. P., 63
Hershey chocolate, 163
Heywood, John, proverbs of, 12
High-altitude cooking, 81
Hindus, forbidden foods, 59

History, food and drink, milestones in, 17, 47, 75, 104, 134, 155, 162–163, 176–177
The History of the Worthies of England (Fuller), 161
Hormel SPAM product, 176
The House at Pooh Corner (Milne), 143
"How the Two Ivans Quarrelled" (Gogol), 104

Ice cream
  Baskin Robbins, 166, 177
  Ben & Jerry's, 177
  flavors, 24
    April Fool's, 116
    Japanese, 123
    statistics, 166
The Importance of Being Earnest (Wilde), 94–95
Indian
  food, 140
  wine pairing and, 34
The Innocents Abroad (Twain), 53
International Federation of Competitive Eating, 90
Irving, Washington, 88
Islamic Duas (supplications), 144
Italian food, 98–99
Ivanoff (Chekhov), 164

Jack Daniel whiskey, 162
Japanese
  food, 33
    brands of, 18
    wine pairing and, 34
  ice cream flavors, 123
  sushi specialties, 112
Jelly beans (Jelly Belly), flavors of, 32
Jerome, Jerome K., 35
Jesus, of Nazareth, 47
Jewish
  blessings, 80
  food, 121
Jews
  forbidden foods, 59
  manna eaten by, 17
Jim Beam Distillery, 155
Johnny Appleseed, 162
Johnson, Samuel, 29, 59
The Journal of a Tour to the Hebrides (Boswell), 29
Joyce, James, 62
Jung, David, 138

Karcher, Carl N., 166
Keats, John, 177
Kellogg's cereal, 163

Kentucky Fried Chicken restaurants, statistics, 167
Keynes, John Maynard, 185
Khan, Kublai, 75
Khayyam, Omar, 14
Korean, food, wine pairing and, 34
Kraft & Bros., 176
Kung pao stir fry, 130

Lagasse, Emeril, 142
Lamb, Charles, 69
Last words, on food and drink, 184–185
Latin American food, 54–55
Lawrence, D. H., 169
Leftovers, 28
"The Legend of Sleepy Hollow" (Irving), 88
Life Is Sweet (movie), 71
The Life of Luxury (Archestratus), 17
The Life of Samuel Johnson (Boswell), 59, 121
Like Water for Chocolate (movie), 72
Lincoln, Abraham, 162
  inaugural luncheon menu, 60
Lipton tea, 163
Little Women (Alcott), 34
Louis IV, King, 75
Louis XIV, King, 130
Love's Labours Lost (Shakespeare), 100
Lucile (Bulwer-Lytton), 153
Lucky Charms breakfast cereal, 142

Madame Bovary (Flaubert), 85
Manners
  poem about, 55
  table, 16–17
Mason jar, 162
Mastering the Art of French Cooking (Child, Beck, Bertholle), 177
Matzoh, origins of, 146
Mayer, Oscar, 163
Mayflower Pilgrims, 134
Mayonnaise, 155
McDonald's restaurants
  founded, 176
  statistics, 166
Measurements, equivalents, 35
Meat
  doneness of, 79
  and seafood, geographic place names, 36
  storage time, 150–152
  taste categories of, 78
Melanesians, forbidden foods, 59
Melba toast, 130
Melitta drip coffee filter, 176
"Le Melon" (de Saint-Amant), 19
Melville, Herman, 59

Menus
  Abraham Lincoln inaugural, 60
  Emperors', 96–97
  on *Titanic*, 82, 168–169
Merckel, Georg, 146
The Merry Wives of Windsor (Shakespeare), 101–102
Metric conversions, 48–49, 84, 118–119
Mexican food, 54–55
Middle Eastern food, 46
A Midsummer's Night's Dream (Shakespeare), 101
Migraine headaches, food triggers, 83
Milne, A. A., 143
Moby Dick (Melville), 58–59
Moët et Chandon, 155
Mongolians, forbidden foods, 59
Montezuma, King, 104
Moonstruck (movie), 70
Moore, Thomas, 162
Mormons, forbidden foods, 59
Moslems, forbidden foods, 59
Mostly Martha (movie), 73
Movies, food and drink in, 70–73
"Murder in the Kitchen" (Toklas), 135
Museum of Comparative Zoology, 78
Museums, food-and-drink-related, 141–142
Musical groups, food-related names of, 111
Mustard
  Colman's, 162
  first powdered, 162
  Grey Poupon, 15
The Mystery of Edwin Drood (Dickens), 23
Mystic Pizza (movie), 71

Nabisco, *see* National Biscuit Company (Nabisco)
Names
  Geographic, *see* Place names (geographic)
  people, famous, 130–131
Napolean III, 162
Napoleon pastry, 130
National Association of Pizza Operators, 166, 167
National Biscuit Company (Nabisco), 163, 176
National Coffee Association, 139
National food observances
  January, 15
  February, 25
  March, 39
  April, 52
  May, 66–67

June, 76
July, 91
August, 108
September, 128
October, 145
November, 160
December, 171
National Pasta Association, 119
Newman, Paul, 177
Newton, Isaac, 134
Nicholas Nickleby (Dickens), 22
North African food, 46
Nutcracker Museum, Leavenworth, 140–141

"Ode to a Nightingale" (Keats), 177
Oliver, Jamie, 142
Oliver Twist (Dickens), 110–111
Omaha Indians, forbidden foods, 59
Orange grove, first, 162
Oscar Mayer weiners, 163
Othello (Shakespeare), 102–103
Oysters, 161
  poem about, 122–123
  statistics, 29

Painter, William, 163
Pan-Asian food, 108–109
Pantry, geographic place names, 77
Parmentier potato dish, 130
Pasta
  shapes of, 64–65
  statistics, 119
Pasteur, Louis, 162
Pavlova dessert, 131
Peach melba, 130
Peanut, George Washington Carver and, 176
Pepper, defying gravity with, 24–25
Pepsi-Cola, 36
Perignon, Dom Pierre, 134, 179
PEZ candy, dispensers, 126–127
The Physiology of Taste (Brillat-Savarin), 162, 184
Picasso, Pablo, 185
"Pig, A Dissertation on Roast" (Lamb), 68–69
Pillsbury flour mill, 163
Pineapples, growing, 105
Pitt, William, 185
Pizarro, Camille, 104
Pizza, statistics, 161, 166, 167
Pizza Hut restaurants, statistics, 167
Place names (geographic)
  alcohol, 56–57
  bakery and pastry, 99

beverage, 135
dairy, 124
meat and seafood, 36
pantry, 77
prepared dishes, 127
produce, 20–21
seasonings and condiments, 170–171
sweets and snacks, 141
Plath, Sylvia, 31
Poe, Edgar Allan, 115
Point, Fernand, 142
Polo, Marco, 75
Ponapeans, forbidden foods, 59
Poor Richard: An Almanack (Franklin), 40, 159
Porridge, 110–111
Portuguese food, 129
Potatoes
  latke, 121
  Parmentier, 130
  statistics, 112
Potter, Beatrix, 77
Pousse café, pouring, 147–149
Prayers
  Christian, 38
  Hindu, 41
  Islamic, 144
  Jewish, 80
Prepared dishes, geographic place names, 127
Pressure cooker, 134
The Price of Milk (movie), 73
Procter & Gamble, 162
Produce, geographic place names, 20–21
Proust, Marcel, 28
Proverbs (Bible), on wine and bread, 172–173
Proverbs (Heywood), 12
Prudhomme, Paul, 142
Puck, Wolfgang, 61
Pythagoras, on salt, 75

Raleigh, Walter Alexander, 55
Ramen Museum, Shin-Yokohama, 141
Reagan, Ronald, 32
Red Sorghum (movie), 71
Remembrance of Things Past (Proust), 28
René, François, 116
Revere, Paul, 155
The Rheinheitsgebot, beer purity law, 113
Robert the Bruce, 185
Romeo and Juliet (Shakespeare), 100
Rourke, Mickey, 70
Rubáiyát (Khayyam), 14
Rueckheim, F. W., 163

Rueckheim, Louis, 163
Russian food, 125
Ruth, George Herman "Babe," 130

Sachertorte, 162
Sainsbury supermarkets, 163
Salad, Receipt for a (Smith), 78
Sanders, Colonel Harland, 167, 177
Sandwich, 131, 155
Scandinavian food, 159
The Scent of Green Papaya (movie), 72
Schlitz brewery, 162
"The Schoolboy's Story" (Dickens), 23
Schueler, Jacob, 163
The Seagull (Chekhov), 165
Seasonings and condiments, geographic place names, 170–171
Seed counts, 57
"The Sermon of the Merry Vicar of Meudon" (de Balzac), 87
Shakespeare, William, food and drink in plays of, 100–103
Simple French Cooking for English Homes (Boulestin), 57
Sirmond, Jean, 161
The Sketch Book of Geoffrey Crayon, Gent. (Irving), 88
Slang
  American diner, 92–94
  Cockney rhyming, 42–45
Smith, Sydney, 78
Soft drinks, statistics, 36
Someone Is Killing the Great Chefs of Europe (Lyons & Lyons), 70
The Sorcerer (Gilbert), 47
Soul Food (movie), 72
Soup
  Campbell's, 163
  chowder, 58–59
  "turtle," 53
SPAM (spiced ham), 176
Spanish food, 129
Specific gravity, of different beverages, 147–149
Squash, history of a, 34
"Stans Puer ad Mensam" (Raleigh), 55
Starbucks coffee, 177
Staton, Joe, 78
Steaks, names of, 116–117
Stockfish Museum, Lofoten, 141
Storage times, refrigerator and freezer, 150–153
Stroganoff, beef, 131
Substitutions in baking, 175

Subway restaurants, statistics, 167
Sushi varieties, 112
Swan Lake (ballet), 131
Sweets and snacks, geographic place names, 141
Swift, Jonathan, 27
Syrup stages, 120

Tabasco hot pepper sauce, 162
Taco Bell restaurants, statistics, 166
The Tale of Peter Rabbit (Potter), 77
The Taming of the Shrew (Shakespeare), 100
Tampopo (movie), 71
Taste (meat), categories of, 78
Tea
  in Japan, 47
  Lipton, 163
  statistics, 139
Temperatures
  boiling point of water, 81
  doneness, 79
  Fahrenheit/Celsius conversion, 118–119
  syrup stages, 120
The Tempest (Shakespeare), 103
Thai, food, wine pairing and, 34
Thanksgiving Day, declared holiday, 162
Thomas, Dylan, 185
Thoreau, Henry David, on kitchen economy, 132–133
Three Men in a Boat (Jerome), 35
Through the Looking Glass (Carroll), 123
Tirel, Guillaume, 75
Titanic
  last dinner menu, 168–169
  last lunch menu, 82
Toll House chocolate chip cookie, 176
Tomatoes, heirloom varieties, 30–31
Tom Jones (movie), 70
Tom Wahl's ice cream shops, 116
Tortilla Soup (movie), 73
A Tramp Abroad (Twain), 50
Treatise on Modern Stimulants (de Balzac), 76
Troilus and Cressida (Shakespeare), 102
Trout, dressing and cooking, 61
Truffles (mushrooms), statistics, 29
Tupperware, 177
Turkish coffee grounds, reading, 174
Turkish food, 46

Twain, Mark, 53, 170
  "little bill of fare," 50–51
Twelfth Night (Shakespeare), 102

Ulysses (Joyce), 62

Le Viander de Taillevent (Tirel), 75
Vietnamese, food, wine pairing and, 34
Vodka, Anton Chekhov on, 164–165

Walden; or, Life in the Woods (Thoreau), 133
A Walk in the Clouds (movie), 72
"The Walrus and the Carpenter" (Carroll), 123
Waring blender, 176
Water
  boiling points of, 81
  bottled, statistics, 21
The Wedding Banquet (movie), 72
Wellington, beef, 131
Wendy's Old Fashioned Hamburgers, statistics, 166
What's Cooking? (movie), 73
White Castle hamburger stands, statistics, 166
Who Is Killing the Great Chefs of Europe? (movie), 70
Wilde, Oscar, 95
Wilhelm I, Kaiser, 96
Wilhelm IV, Duke, 104, 113
Williams-Sonoma stores, 177
Willy Wonka and the Chocolate Factory (movie), 70
The Wind in the Willows (Grahame), 12
Wine
  Ben Franklin's tips on making, 158–159
  biblical proverbs concerning, 172–173
  food pairing and, 34
  industry, Californian, 162
  properties and effects of, 146
  terms pertaining to, 67
The Winter's Tale (Shakespeare), 103
Woman on Top (movie), 73
Women in Love (Lawrence), 169
World records, eating, 90–91

Yellow Submarine (movie), 114–115